Choose to Forgive

Choose to Forgive

Discovering the Life-Transforming Power of Forgiveness

STEVE SCHOTT

Copyright © 2022 by Steve Schott

Choose to Forgive: Discovering the Life-Transforming Power of Forgiveness

All rights reserved. No part of this publication may be reproduced, distributed, or transmitted in any form or by any means, including photocopying, recording, or other electronic or mechanical methods, without the prior written permission of the publisher, except in the case of brief quotations embodied in critical reviews and certain other noncommercial uses permitted by copyright law.

Although the author and publisher have made every effort to ensure that the information in this book was correct at press time, the author and publisher do not assume and hereby disclaim any liability to any party for any loss, damage, or disruption caused by errors or omissions, whether such errors or omissions result from negligence, accident, or any other cause.

Unless otherwise indicated, all Scripture quotations are from the ESV® Bible (The Holy Bible, English Standard Version®), copyright © 2001 by Crossway, a publishing ministry of Good News Publishers. Used by permission. All rights reserved. You may not copy or download more than 500 consecutive verses of the ESV Bible or more than one half of any book of the ESV Bible.

Adherence to all applicable laws and regulations, including international, federal, state, and local governing professional licensing, business practices, advertising, and all other aspects of doing business in the U.S., Canada, or any other jurisdiction is the sole responsibility of the reader and consumer.

Neither the author nor the publisher assumes any responsibility or liability whatsoever on behalf of the consumer or reader of this material. Any perceived slight of any individual or organization is purely unintentional.

The resources in this book are provided for informational purposes only and should not be used to replace the specialized training and professional judgment of a health care or mental health care professional.

Neither the author nor the publisher can be held responsible for the use of the information provided within this book. Please always consult a trained professional before making any decision regarding treatment of yourself or others.

ISBN: 979-8-986-22220-2

CONTENTS

INTRODUCTION	1
CHAPTER 1 Forgive to Live—The Healing Power of Forgiveness	11
CHAPTER 2 Why Forgive?—Because the Bible Tells Me So	23
CHAPTER 3 What Is Forgiveness?	33
CHAPTER 4 How Can I Possibly Forgive This?	43
CHAPTER 5 Hidden Unforgiveness— Detecting Unforgiveness Hiding In Your Heart	53
CHAPTER 6 Forgive Thyself	67
CHAPTER 7 Accepting Forgiveness	77

CHAPTER 8	85
Love Is All You Need	
CHAPTER 9	97
The Power of Prayer	
CHAPTER 10	105
The Ugly Truth About Anger	
CHAPTER 11	119
How to Apologize … And Mean It!	
CHAPTER 12	139
Ten Dangerous Myths	
CONCLUSION	145
APPENDIX A	149
41 Inspirational Quotes	
APPENDIX B	155
Key Scripture Verses on Forgiveness	
REFERENCES	171
ACKNOWLEDGMENTS	179
CAN YOU HELP?	183

INTRODUCTION

"Blessed is the one whose transgressions are forgiven, whose sins are covered." –Psalm 32:1

*I've been tryin' to get down
To the heart of the matter
But my will gets weak
And my thoughts seem to scatter
But I think it's about
Forgiveness, Forgiveness
Even if, even if you don't love me anymore.*

– The Heart of the Matter, Don Henley, 1989

People have asked, "Why are you writing a book on forgiveness?" The braver ones have inquired, "What do you even know about forgiveness?" The cynics say, "Does the world really need another book about forgiveness?"

Good questions, and I am always grateful when they ask. Allow me to answer them for you.

There are outstanding books written on the subject of forgiveness. There are also excellent materials on the Internet covering this topic.

What struck me, however, was the literature primarily focuses on one of two subjects: (a) what medicine and science have to say about forgiveness, or (b) what the Bible says about forgiveness. So, my thought was, why not one book that explores both subjects?

Also, the great majority of these books and articles are written for and directed to individuals who have suffered major trauma or injury. They fall into various self-help categories, including personal memoirs, that all deal with how someone overcame a terrible ordeal through the power of forgiveness.

You will experience this in the stories included in this book. These stories focus on "forgiving the unforgivable." Everyone, however, needs to learn to forgive. We all struggle daily with situations that frustrate or anger us, creating moments in time that merit a spirit of forgiveness.

In one sense, this book is directed at readers who recognize the need to forgive but who lack the knowledge or experience to help them do it. In another sense, this book is intended for those who don't recognize the need to forgive nor feel inclined to do so. After all, what's the big deal, right?

As we will learn, however, it is a really big deal. In fact, it can be a life-transforming deal.

However, the reason you are reading this book at all, as mysterious as it may sound, is that God told me to write it. There, I said it.

Confession time. I harbor a secret jealousy towards those who claim to hear from God on a regular basis. I have secretly

INTRODUCTION

wanted to say to them, "Maybe if you stopped hogging all of God's time, He would have time to speak to me!"

I never heard God speak to me before. If He was speaking to me, I apparently did not have my God-listening ears on. Until one night in February 2021 (about the time Winter Storm Uri swept through Texas).

As I lay sleeping (I would have been terrified if this happened while I was awake), I had a dream. In this dream, I heard God speaking directly to me. In fact, we had a short conversation (which is how I imagine most conversations with God have gone through the ages—short and to the point). The conversation went something like this:

God: "I want you to write a book."
Steve: "Me? A book? I am not an author."
God: "You are now. I want you to write a book for me."
Steve: "On what?"
God: "I want you to write a book on forgiveness."
Steve: "Forgiveness? I don't know the first thing about forgiveness."
God: "Exactly. Now write the book."

That was the extent of our conversation. Even though I am sure I had many, many questions, God had nothing further to say. However, as John Stickl, the pastor at my home church, Valley Creek, says, "God speaks in sentences, not paragraphs."

Unlike Samuel, who finally responded, "Speak, Lord, your servant hears" (1 Samuel 3:10), I awoke the next morning and did ... nothing. Oh, I vividly remembered the dream, and it replayed in my head. But I dismissed the thought and chalked it up to eating ice cream too late the night before.

A few days later, I was at church and mentioned the dream to Jason Hillier, the Campus Pastor at Valley Creek. His response just made me laugh: "Well then, I guess you have a book to write." Yeah, right.

Months went by, and I never heard from God again on the subject. But lo-and-behold, if coincidental things didn't start happening. While driving in my car, I turned on the radio and heard the song "Heart of the Matter" come on. As I typically do when I hear a song I am familiar with, I sang along (alone, in my car, with the windows rolled up is the only place in the world safe for me to sing). I sang the lyrics from memory, not really paying much attention to the words. However, each time I got to the chorus, it struck me more and more that one word kept getting used, what Mr. Henley was calling "the heart of the matter," forgiveness. I remember thinking, "Interesting."

I should have mentioned that I rarely listen to the car radio anymore. I prefer silence when I am driving (just ask any passenger in my car). God only knows why I turned on the radio at that moment.

I'd like to say that this realization hit me like a ton of bricks dropped from above (as in way, way above), and that I immediately turned my car around, went home, and started working on the book. But you already know the answer to that.

A short while later, an online devotional did a brief series about … forgiveness. That got my attention, sort of. I made a mental note to save the series in a file just in case I might need it someday. I only wish I could remember where I had saved it.

Two more months went by and still no book. I had recently become a newly appointed member of a local board responsible

INTRODUCTION

for hearing disputes between the appraisal district and property owners over the appraised value of their property. This is a big deal in Texas, because property taxes are based on the assessed value of personal and real property. One day, as we were hearing property value protests, a member on my panel suddenly turned to me and handed me a little card. She said, "I like to hand out these random Bible cards to people." I read the card:

"I pray that you will be kind, compassionate, and forgiving of others, just as God forgave you through Christ. – Ephesians 4:32"

To put this in perspective, I had already gained a bit of a reputation as a strict, no nonsense, follow the rules decision-maker, which often put me at odds with other members. So, my first thought was that this person just didn't like the way I was running the hearing that day. But there was one word on this card that caught my attention. So, when she said, "If you don't like that card, I can give you a different one," I said, "No, I will keep this one." In the back of my mind, I was starting to think the card might come in handy.

About one month later, our church started a new sermon series on building relationships. In the first sermon on this series, Pastor Jason preached on what he referred to as "a cornerstone of healthy relationships." I am sure you can guess what he was talking about. As for me, I remember thinking, "I probably should take some notes on what he is saying and read his scripture references. I might need them."

The following day, I received a completely unsolicited email inviting me to a free seminar on how to self-publish a book. I watched the webinar and even signed up for the free, no-obligation exploratory telephone consultation. You know, the one that ends with the hard sell to buy the offering. When the time for the call came, I decided I would not answer the phone. Whew, dodged that bullet. But wouldn't you know, the consultant left a message, requesting I call him. And then I heard a Holy whisper, "Call him back."

I did.

Two days later, I started this book.

Now you know how this guide to forgiveness came into existence. But what about the book content?

As I stated, the majority of available literature on forgiveness is directed at people who have suffered a major life trauma. You will certainly see this in the stories I share, but what about the daily slings and arrows of life and their impact on our feelings and emotions such as anger or bitterness? And what about our ability to manage that anger, and ultimately, our ability and willingness to forgive? Simple daily situations we all encounter:

- Mistreatment by a co-worker
- Working for a terrible boss
- Friends and family being unsupportive when you need them
- Bad financial decisions you have made because of being misled by someone
- Traffic
- Polarizing politics
- The daily news

INTRODUCTION

This book explores how to choose the ability and willingness to forgive the big and little frustrations we all face and experience every day. We will explore the why, what, and how of forgiveness, including self-forgiveness. We will address struggles many people have with accepting forgiveness or acknowledging when they have been forgiven and what that means.

We will also uncover the superpowers that are key to adopting an attitude of forgiveness—turns out The Beatles were right!

The book will touch upon the thorny issue of anger, which typically serves as both the cause of the wrongdoing that requires forgiveness and the inability of some of us to forgive. We will also learn the importance of saying—and how to say—"I'm sorry." Unfortunately, apologizing is a skill that most of us have never been taught.

We will conclude our journey with a brief look at some common myths surrounding anger and forgiveness. I have also included a list of inspirational quotes and Bible verses to help you remember what this forgiveness thing is all about. Please refer to them whenever you need a reminder!

Before we start, I want to share a personal story that, frankly, I had forgotten until starting to write this book. I grew up with what you would call a normal childhood free of major trauma or drama. About the worst that happened was the death of several pets over the years—some from old age and natural causes, others from being in the wrong street at the wrong time.

But one thing missing from my childhood was love, or at least the open expression of love. We were a performance-based family; you were recognized when you performed. This was particularly true of my father. Rarely would we experience or witness an actual expression of love. I think we felt loved, but rarely did we hear anyone say, "I love you" or see any outward expression of love.

In fact, the one time my father tried to show some affection occurred at a family party when I was in my teen years. After being chided by my mother, "You never hug me anymore," my father suddenly and without warning gave my mother a big hug. The real surprise was the two ribs he broke with his hug. Her ribs, not his. Needless to say, my mother never asked my father for another hug, and for the most part, that was the end of hugs in our family (unless you were a cat or a dog or maybe a pet goldfish).

Many years later, I travelled to California to visit my father when he was hospitalized for a serious heart attack (not sure why that word is used—aren't all heart attacks serious?). At the end of my final visit at the hospital with my mother and father, my mother turned to my father and said, "Tell Steve that you love him." To which my father responded, "He knows I love him." I mumbled something similar in return when I felt like saying, "No I don't!"

Along with this absence of any real expression of love in our family, there was a dearth of apologizing and forgiving. Mostly we just went forward in life with hurts and emotional bruises intact. This should not surprise you. As we will learn, love—especially love manifested—is a key component of forgiveness.

I believe, in his own way, my father loved me. But after researching and writing this book, I also believe that the absence of expressed love and affection in our house nurtured me into becoming a performance-driven, demanding person. I demanded a lot of myself and others. The failure of others to live up to my expectations led me to become judgmental and less forgiv-

INTRODUCTION

ing. Confession time: This book is for me as much as it is for you! I think that is the real reason God wanted me to write it.

This book thus explores different facets of the complex subject of forgiveness. Each chapter is intended to build upon each preceding chapter; however, you should feel free to jump to a specific chapter that is of particular interest to you. I encourage you, however, to read the entire book. Doing so will give you a more complete understanding of a complex subject, helping you to discover and grasp the truly life-changing, life-saving power of forgiveness.

CHAPTER 1

Forgive to Live—The Healing Power of Forgiveness

"Be kind and compassionate to one another, forgiving each other, just as in Christ God forgave you." – Ephesians 4:32

"Forgive others, not because they deserve forgiveness, but because you deserve peace." – Mel Robbins

Brooks Douglass was 16 when two armed men entered his family home while his mom was cooking dinner. The men proceeded to hog-tie Brooks and his parents in their living room, taking his pre-teen sister into another room and repeatedly raping her. Brooks and his parents could do nothing but listen to her scream for over three hours. After they had finished torturing the little girl, the attackers sat down and ate the family dinner while debating what to do next. When they finished the family's dinner, the two men shot Brooks, his sister, and both of his parents. His mother and father died within minutes. Brooks and his sister survived and escaped, driving to a neighbor for help. They were hospitalized, under police guard for three weeks, and then moved in with friends.

Over the next fifteen years, Brooks testified nine times at trials and clemency hearings for the two men who had destroyed his family—having to re-live the nightmare over and over. Brooks found his life in a downward spiral of alcohol abuse, depression, and repeated failures.

Brooks eventually graduated from college, earned a law degree, and became the youngest state senator in Oklahoma history. From the outside, it appeared he had finally gotten his life together, but on the inside, anger and rage were tearing him apart.

As a Christian, Douglass understood what the Bible has to say about forgiveness. However, he admits he was unprepared to forgive the men who murdered his parents and raped his sister: "I know that it's something that I should do, and I know it's something my parents would want me to do, so, more or less, I said, 'Lord, I'm not ready, but I'm willing to be made ready, down the line.'"

In 1995, as a state senator, Brooks toured the Oklahoma State Penitentiary, where one of his attackers was imprisoned for life. Later, admitting he did not understand what came over him, Brooks asked the prison warden for permission to visit the imprisoned attacker. The warden initially refused but relented under pressure from the state senator. So, at his insistence, Brooks came face to face with his attacker. After speaking with the man for over an hour, Douglass got up to leave and then said to the man who had viciously raped his sister and murdered his parents, "I forgive you."

Brooks Douglass said of that moment, "And then I remember feeling like someone had taken a clamp off my chest and I could breathe for the first time in 15 years." He continued, "I didn't really understand it that much at that moment, but I knew that the only way I was going to get up and walk out of that room and be able to start dealing with other things in my life was by forgiving him."[1]

"I don't get mad; I get even."

A popular mantra for some, "I don't get mad; I get even," is often uttered in response to some slight—real or imagined—committed against them. It has become a way of automatic thinking for many whenever they feel someone has done them wrong.

Psychologists say that this mantra of "get even" reflects an attitude and mindset of revenge that is equally harmful whether or not actually carried out. This mindset of revenge says, "You have wronged me, and I am going to pay you back for the wrong."

So, what's the big deal, right? After all, most of us don't actually carry out our revenge. We may fantasize about it, and we may even fantasize about how we will get even, but about the only thing we really get is mad. And we stay that way.

What is the solution, then? Stay mad? As we will discover, staying in revenge mode has serious, life-threatening consequences. In this chapter, we will discover why you need to adopt an attitude and mindset of forgiveness to enjoy a life well-lived.

---

1   Smith, Tim. "Brooks Douglass: Strength to Forgive." CBN.com. https://www1.cbn.com/700club/brooks-douglass-strength-forgive

Live Better, Live Longer

Our journey to adopting a spirit of forgiveness starts with the question, "Why forgive?" As a concession to basic human nature, consider this the answer to the corollary question, "What's in it for me?"

What you will discover is that the mindset of "getting even" has serious mental, emotional, and physical consequences that not only affect your health but might dictate just how long you live! That's right, a mindset of unforgiveness can actually lead to a shorter, unhealthy life. (Especially, I suppose, if your act of revenge doesn't go as planned!) What you will learn is that the only person you are really hurting with your anger and vengeful mindset is yourself!

Forgiveness, in psychological terms, is an emotional and cognitive process characterized by a release of anger leading to peace of mind. The renowned Christian author and theologian, Lewis B. Smedes, warns us, "To forgive is to set a prisoner free and discover that the prisoner was you."

Studies have found that the act of forgiveness can reap huge rewards for your health. These studies show that people who hang on to grudges are more likely to experience severe depression and post-traumatic stress disorder, as well as other health conditions. "There is an enormous physical burden to being hurt and disappointed," says Karen Swartz, M.D., director of the Mood Disorders Adult Consultation Clinic at The Johns Hopkins Hospital.[2]

---

2   "Forgiveness: Your Health Depends on It." John Hopkins Medicine. https://www.hopkinsmedicine.org/health/wellness-and-prevention/forgiveness-your-health-depends-on-it

CHAPTER 1

Chronic anger puts you into a fight-or-flight mode, which results in numerous changes in heart rate, blood pressure, and immune response. Those changes increase the risk of depression, heart disease, and diabetes, among other conditions. According to Dr. Swartz, "Forgiveness, however, calms stress levels, leading to improved health." In fact, studies have also found that people who are just naturally more forgiving tend to be more satisfied with their lives and have less depression, anxiety, stress, anger, and hostility.

In a 2004 study by Worthington and Scheer, the inability or unwillingness to forgive was linked to unresolved anger and hostility, which were proven to have negative health effects, particularly on cardiovascular health. By comparison, the study linked forgiveness to positive emotions of empathy and compassion, which led to positive effects on physical, emotional, and mental health.[3]

Another study revealed that holding a grudge, repeatedly reliving painful memories, and harboring deep-seated resentment had a negative impact on individual health and well-being and that unforgiveness contributed to coronary heart disease.

In short, a willingness to forgive can lead to:

- Healthier relationships
- Greater psychological well-being
- Less anxiety, stress, and hostility
- Lower blood pressure

---

[3] Worthington, Everett, L. Jr. "The New Science of Forgiveness." Greater Good Magazine (1 September 2004): https://greatergood.berkeley.edu/article/item/the_new_science_of_forgiveness

- Fewer symptoms of depression
- Stronger immune system
- Improved heart health
- Longevity

Living with a spirit of unforgiveness makes you a prisoner of poor health, anxiety, stress, depression, and other physical and psychological distress, and could even shorten your life. Given the choice, the question we need to ask ourselves is, "Why not forgive?"

The emotional consequences of unforgiveness can be equally damaging. Studies have shown that an inability to forgive can:

- Lead to anger and bitterness becoming a part of every relationship and new experience
- Leave you feeling so trapped in the past wrong you cannot enjoy the present or look forward to the future
- Cause you to feel that life lacks meaning or purpose
- Create feelings of guilt and doubt because it puts you at odds with your spiritual beliefs
- Result in the loss of valuable and enriching connectedness with others and even with yourself
- Leave you feeling emotionally drained and exhausted from the extra energy it takes to hold a grudge or desire for revenge

Most important to consider is research that shows that people who adopt a spirit of unconditional forgiveness may actually live longer. In one of the first research projects to study the impact of forgiveness on longevity, researchers determined that the one quality of forgiveness that predicted mortality was conditional versus unconditional forgiveness of others.[4]

The research, conducted by Luther College psychologist Loren Toussaint and colleagues and published in the *Journal of Behavioral Medicine*, found that people high on the scale of conditional forgiveness, meaning they will only forgive others on conditional terms, died before people who scored low on this measure. People who practiced unconditional forgiveness, extending forgiveness without expecting or demanding anything in return, outlived those who were unwilling to forgive unless certain conditions (an apology, restitution, etc.) were first met.

The researchers concluded that people who make demands for forgiveness continue to harbor resentment and grudges, emotions that can impair their heart's health. Continually nursing those negative feelings keeps stress levels high, and it's this stress that ultimately exacts its payment in the form of early death.

The moral of the story? Forgive if you want to live!

Forgiveness = Healthy Relationships = Longevity

Another aspect of forgiveness that affects our mortality is the impact of forgiveness, or unforgiveness, on the health of our relationships. Studies have shown that as we get older, the quality of our relationships has a direct impact on how long we might live. Other studies reveal that the quality of our relationships is dependent on our ability and willingness to forgive.

---

[4] Toussaint, L.L., Owen, A.D. & Cheadle, A. Forgive to Live: Forgiveness, Health, and Longevity. *J Behav Med* 35, 375–386 (2012). https://doi.org/10.1007/s10865-011-9362-4

In his book, *Timeless: Nature's Formula for Health and Longevity*, Louis Cozolino, professor of psychology at Pepperdine University, emphasizes the positive impact of human relationships. "Of all the experiences we need to survive and thrive, it is the experience of relating to others that is the most meaningful and important," he writes.[5]

Professor Cozolino states that our brains are social organs, meaning we are wired to connect with each other and to interact in groups. He concludes that a life that maximizes social interaction and human-to-human contact is good for the brain at every stage, particularly for the aging brain. He concludes that, "People who lead extraordinarily long lives are those who have maintained close ties to others."

By its very nature, our lack of willingness to forgive is a form of alienation between us and the person we are unwilling or unable to forgive. It creates discord between us and them and, in effect, creates an invisible barrier blocking the path to a healthy relationship.

This might be okay if the offending person is some stranger on the freeway (although the root cause of our anger undoubtedly manifests itself in all relationships), but when our anger erupts towards our spouse, our children, family members, friends, co-workers, and others we interact with daily, the lack of forgiveness that grows out of that anger will negatively affect that relationship in almost every way, leading to an unhealthy relationship. The unhealthier our relationships, the sooner we may die!

---

5   Cozolino, Louis J. *Timeless: Nature's Formula for Health and Longevity*. W.W. Norton & Company, 2018.

CHAPTER 1

For the person who is always angry or resentful, chances are that anger and resentment manifest themselves in every relationship and every situation that doesn't go the way they want or think it should go. Chances are high that these folks are completely lacking in healthy relationships.

Numerous studies suggest that people who can forgive evidence greater quality in their relationships with others and a greater commitment to those relationships, while people who demonstrate strong motivation for revenge and avoidance have significantly lower relationship satisfaction.

A 2017 study set out to determine the effect on personal well-being of individuals who appeared to be predisposed towards having a forgiving nature. The study referred to this as "state forgiveness" or the intentional, purpose-driven disposition bent towards forgiveness. The study concluded that individuals who experience this "state forgiveness" perceived a greater sense of mental well-being, which included experiencing positive relationships with others and identification of a sense of purpose and meaning in life.[6]

At the risk of repeating myself, let me again say the research is rather conclusive on this point. Unforgiveness can lead to a premature death![7] I would suggest that wherever you may be in your life, now is the time to repair your relationships through the daily practice of unconditional forgiveness. Do not wait until

---

6   Akhtar, S., Dolan, A. & Barlow, J. Understanding the Relationship Between State Forgiveness and Psychological Wellbeing: A Qualitative Study. *J Relig Health* **56,** 450–463 (2017). https://doi.org/10.1007/s10943-016-0188-9

7   Whitbourne, Susan Krauss, PhD. "Live Longer by Practicing Forgiveness." (1 January 2013). https://www.psychologytoday.com/us/blog/fulfillment-any-age/201301/live-longer-practicing-forgiveness.

you are on your deathbed to forgive the people in your life. Especially when unforgiveness in your heart may lead you to that final resting place sooner than you would prefer.

Next Steps—Start Your Journey to Forgiveness

You now have a better understanding of the life-transforming benefits associated with adopting an attitude of forgiveness. And you now understand those benefits are real. However, if you are like me (and most people), it is the "how to" that frustrates you. As in, "I understand what forgiveness can do for me, but how do I start forgiving?"

Fortunately, there are several immediate actions you can take to begin the process of transforming your well-being through the power of forgiveness. As you consider your answers to the question "Why should I forgive," consider taking the following steps as you embark on the forgiveness journey:

1. Identify one area of unforgiven hurt or anger in your life that really stands out. There may be more than one, but for now just choose one. (Hint: You can repeat this exercise over and over for each hurt!)

2. Ask yourself:

a. In the light of the passage of time, how badly was I hurt (perhaps use a scale of 1–10, with 1 being really not that bad and 10 being absolutely horrible)?
b. What is the root of that hurt?
c. How has it affected my relationship with that person?

d. To what extent has the hurt negatively affected my physical, mental, or emotional well-being?
e. To what extent has unforgiven hurt affected my relationship with others?
f. What could my life look like if I were to stop drinking this poison?
g. Am I willing to at least consider extending forgiveness in this situation even though undeserved?

Health benefits and longevity are practical reasons to consider forgiveness as a way of life. But there is another aspect to forgiveness that lies at the root of the question, "Why forgive?" In the next section, we will explore the reasons to forgive from a Biblical perspective. Whether you consider yourself a Christian or not, the concepts of forgiveness rooted in historical Christianity apply to everyone.

CHAPTER 2

Why Forgive?—Because the Bible Tells Me So

"Bear with each other and forgive one another if any of you has a grievance against someone. Forgive as the Lord forgave you." – Colossians 3:13

"Not forgiving someone is like drinking poison and expecting the other person to die."
– Nelson Mandela

On November 5, 2003, Gary Ridgway, referred to as the "Green River Killer," pled guilty in a Seattle courtroom to murdering 48 teenage girls and women, a 49th murder victim was added as part of his plea bargain (life in prison without the possibility of parole). In all, he confessed to 71 murders. As he pled guilty one by one to each murder, Ridgway showed absolutely no regret or remorse. In statements given to the police, he claimed he had no memory of any of the women he had killed, stating "they didn't mean anything to me."

At his sentencing hearing on December 18, 2003, family members of the victims had the opportunity to speak directly to Ridgway, who sat completely stone-faced as family member after family member condemned him for what he had done to their loved ones. "I wish for him to have a long suffering, cruel death," said one grieving speaker. Another said, "He's going to Hell, and that's where he belongs." The statements continued along this vein until Robert Rule, the father of one of his victims, took his turn at the podium. He began with, "Mr. Ridgway, there are people here that hate you." Then, after he long pause, he stated simply, "I'm not one of them." At this, Ridgway's facial expression began to change. Mr. Rule continued, "You have made it difficult to live up to what I believe, and that is what God says to do. And that's to forgive." After another brief pause, Mr. Rule, looking directly at Ridgway, simply said, "You are forgiven, sir." And with that, the man who had showed absolutely no emotion during his conviction or sentencing procedures broke into tears, visibly moved by this one simple act of forgiveness.[8]

Power of Forgiveness

The power of forgiveness, evidenced in Ridgway's response to one father's act of forgiveness, lies at the core of the Christian faith. There are approximately 100 verses in the Bible that deal with forgiveness, 68 of which appear throughout the New Testament. The total of these verses teaches two powerful lessons: We are to forgive others as God has forgiven us—not because they

---

8   "Serial Killer Cries Over Father's Forgiveness." (5 October 2012). https://www.youtube.com/watch?v=iY8iWJ5h5aM

deserve it, but because forgiveness is rooted in love, and love demands we forgive others for what they have done.

Over the years, there has been philosophical debate over whether the modern concept of forgiveness originated with Christianity. It is an interesting debate, but in many respects, it is simply comparing apples to oranges. While the basic concept of forgiveness appears in the Jewish precepts of the Old Testament and in other religious and pagan belief systems, the concept of undeserved forgiveness based on love, mercy, and grace is uniquely Christian in its origin.

Under the tenets of most non-Christian philosophies, forgiveness is a one-way street from the deity to humans, and it is something that must be earned and may or may not be extended, depending on the vagaries of the offended god.

While there are multiple references to forgiveness in the Old Testament (see, for example, Numbers 4:19–21), they reflect the forgiveness of God towards his people. However, when it comes to a spirit of forgiveness between people, human to human, if you will, the prevailing attitude was revenge: an eye for an eye, a tooth for a tooth (see Leviticus 24:19–21). The prevailing spirit was personal retaliation, to seek and achieve revenge for the offense or slight. This concept was flipped on its head under the new paradigm pronounced by Jesus.

God's Command to Forgive

In Matthew's Gospel, Jesus repudiated the idea of personal retaliation and ushered in a spirit of forgiveness:

"You have heard that it was said, 'An eye for an eye and a tooth for a tooth.' But I say to you, Do not resist the one who is

evil. But if anyone slaps you on the right cheek, turn to him the other also." –Matthew 5:38–39

One can imagine how radical this sounded to the people of this time. Prior to Jesus' call to forgive, the cultural norm was to expect and even demand personal revenge for a committed offense. Jesus, however, tells His listeners that they are not to retaliate but rather, they should seek to forgive others even if these individuals do not deserve forgiveness!

At its root, the "turn the other cheek" philosophy presented by Jesus is a reminder that God calls us to forgive, not because someone has earned or deserved our forgiveness, but because that is what God wants and has commanded us to do. This makes the concept of *unearned* forgiveness uniquely Christian.

Consider the ultimate act of forgiveness. With his dying breaths on the cross, Jesus asked God to, "ForgiveHH them for they know not what they do" (Luke 23:34). Jesus wasn't asking God to forgive his persecutors and executioners because they deserved forgiveness. Instead, he asked for forgiveness from a place of unselfish love. Human nature being what it is, forgiveness matters only when it is extended unconditionally from a spirit of love. Author and Pastor Judah Smith concludes that with this final prayer, Jesus revealed His essence, that He is "the personification of God's unconditional love and forgiveness."[9]

Forgiving others is what God has called us to do: "Forgive us our debts, as we also have forgiven our debtors" (Matthew 6:12). This passage implies that God forgives us in direct proportion to the forgiveness we extend to others. We are forgiven by the

---

9   Smith, Judah. *How's Your Soul: Why Everything that Matters Starts with the Inside You.* Nelson Books, 2016.

grace of God, and, because of that forgiveness, God expects us to extend that same grace to others in a spirit of forgiveness.

Unfortunately, it goes against our human nature to forgive others. At the root of this challenge is an extreme focus on self. We focus so much on what has been done to us and how it affects our needs and desires that we cannot see past ourselves to forgive.

Selfishness is a much more natural human response than graciousness. Have you ever been stuck in a long line at the grocery store checkout with what you perceive to be a slow check-out clerk or bagger? Do you see this as an interruption to your plans for the day? That is how a selfish spirit might view the situation. Selfishness leads to anger. Grace, on the other hand, would stop to consider whether the person is struggling to keep his job. Or that perhaps she recently received the worst news of her life.

Grace paves the way for forgiveness. Grace is not, however, a natural human response. It flows to us from God, and it is that flow of grace that allows us to "turn the other cheek" and forgo the selfishness that leads to anger and resentment and to instead choose to forgive.

That guy that cuts you off on the freeway or, heaven forbid, changes lanes in front of you without putting on his blinker? You do not know what he might be going through. But the one thing you do know is that he, like you, needs God's love. You can show him some of that grace that you have been blessed with by forgiving him for whatever affront you think he has committed. And get on with your day free of that anger.

Unforgiveness will keep you stuck in the past. If you cannot forgive, you will not enjoy God's vision for your life. You cannot see the way forward when your eyes are focused on your rearview mirror.

Forgive and get on with your life. This doesn't mean there shouldn't be consequences for what somebody did to you. It just means that you let go of your anger and hurt and give it to God so that you can move forward with God's purpose for your life.

The Strength to Forgive

People often ask, "How can I find the strength to forgive? I don't have it in me." None of us can do it entirely on our own. Keep in mind that the process of forgiving will not be linear. There will be starts, stops, and backwards steps as you travel the road to forgiveness. As a believer, the only place you will find the strength to engage in forgiveness is remembering how much you have been forgiven. It is remembering that we have been forgiven that we find the strength and grace to forgive others.

In the book *Calm My Anxious Heart: A Woman's Guide to Finding Contentment* by Linda Dillow, there is a brief story about Clara Barton, the founder of the American Red Cross. This story teaches us that forgiveness is a choice.

One day, a friend reminded Clara of a vicious deed that someone had done to her years before. But she acted as if she had never heard of the incident! "Don't you remember it?" her friend asked. "No," came Clara's reply, "I distinctly remember forgetting it." She had made a conscious choice to forgive a vicious deed, a conscious choice to continue forgiving when reminded of the deed. By replying, "I distinctly remember forgetting it," Clara Barton was saying,

CHAPTER 2

"I remember choosing to forgive, and I still choose to forgive."[10]

But what about things that appear absolutely unforgivable? How are we supposed to find the strength to forgive in those situations? These are the painful places where the idea of forgiveness can seem impossible.

In Luke 17:3–4, Jesus says, "If your brother or sister sins against you, rebuke them; and if they repent, forgive them. Even if they sin against you seven times in a day and seven times come back to you saying, 'I repent,' you must forgive them."

The message is unequivocal: we should not withhold forgiveness, no matter the situation. We can rebuke the perpetrator. We can seek to bring them to justice and even rejoice when they receive the justice they deserve. Actions have worldly consequences, so it is only right and fair that wrong actions have consequences for the person who commits them.

Forgiveness, however, requires us to look past our desire to seek justice. As we said earlier, the act of forgiving someone who has hurt you is a matter of the heart. Forgiveness is the practice of seeing others as broken people whom God formed in His own image. When you consider this in all its mysterious splendor, how can we stay angry at someone whom God created? This concept lies at the core of the ability of people like Brooks Douglass and Robert Rule to forgive the men who murdered their loved ones.

When forgiveness seems impossible and you feel like you can't be gracious toward someone and forgive them, just re-

---

[10] Dillow, Linda. *Calm My Anxious Heart: A Woman's Guide to Finding Contentment.* NavPress, 2007.

member that Jesus has forgiven you. You have been forgiven by your Creator for every transgression you have committed or will ever commit. When I think of my own transgressions, I imagine Jesus on the cross, saying, "Father, forgive Steve, for he knows not what he is doing."

If Jesus could forgive me as He was being crucified, who am I to refuse to forgive others for their transgressions against me? You want an answer to "Why forgive?" You have it in the person of Jesus Christ.

Next Steps—Forgive From a Spirit of Forgiveness

God's Word teaches us why we must forgive and the power of adopting a spirit of forgiveness in our daily interactions with other people. The Bible leaves no doubt that we are forgiven by our Creator, and, because of this forgiveness, we need to forgive others.

Biblical forgiveness, however, can prove challenging. For many of us, Biblical truths sound good but are difficult to actually put into action. As you consider the "why forgive" question from God's point of view, consider engaging in the following self-examination to better understand and appreciate the call to forgive.

1. Do I accept the truth that I am forgiven by God? If the answer is no, why not?
2. Thinking back to the one area of unforgiven hurt or anger in my life identified in Chapter 1, do I believe God's command to forgive as I have been forgiven can apply to this transgression?
3. In what way have I allowed my emotions and feelings to

come between me and God's command to forgive?
4. Ask God to help you understand why you need to forgive this person or situation and to help you take your next step towards ultimately being able to forgive.

Understanding the "why" of forgiveness is a critical first step on the journey to adopting a spirit of forgiveness. Once we understand why we should forgive and learn to appreciate its impact on our physical, emotional, mental, and spiritual health as well as our longevity, we move forward to understand what forgiveness means and how we can adopt a spirit of forgiveness.

CHAPTER 3

What Is Forgiveness?

"If your enemy is hungry, feed him; if he is thirsty, give him something to drink; for by so doing, you will heap burning coals on his head." – Romans 12:20

"To be wronged is nothing unless you continue to remember it."
– Confucius

forgiveness
[ˌfərˈgivnəs]
NOUN
   1. the action or process of forgiving or being forgiven

The simplicity in the definition of the word "forgiveness" hides the complexity inherent in the process of forgiving someone. This makes for a daunting challenge to understand, let alone engage in, forgiveness.

Dr. Steven Marmer of UCLA Medical School concludes, "One of our challenges in understanding this process is that the word—forgiveness—is inadequate to explain a very complex

concept." He believes that the idea of forgiveness "actually embodies three different things, each of which applies to different situations and provides different results."[11]

Dr. Marmer identifies three basic types of forgiveness:

- Exoneration
- Forbearance
- Release

Exoneration, he explains, involves "wiping the slate clean" and fully restoring the relationship as if nothing ever happened. Think of a child who does something wrong without even realizing it. When the child tells you he is sorry, you quickly forgive the child and continue with the relationship as if it never happened. Dr. Marmer states that in such situations, it is important to accept an apology if one is warranted and given and offer complete exoneration for the offense.

Forbearance, he says, is a bit more complicated. Forbearance is forgiveness in response to a partial apology or an apology commingled with a suggestion that you are at least partly to blame. Often, the apology given is inauthentic or at least not offered unconditionally. In these situations, Dr. Marmer warns, if the relationship matters to you, forbearance would be an appropriate response. You don't really forgive as much as you decide to just move on from the situation.

Release, however, neither exonerates nor forbears. It does not even require a continuation or restoration of a broken re-

---

11   Marmer, Stephen Dr. M.D. (05 May 2014). https://www.prageru.com/video/forgiveness

lationship. Dr. Marmer concludes that in a situation calling for release, you must decide to cease dwelling on the pain and anger that is holding you back and "choose to move forward" without this past burden weighing you down.

The type of forgiveness Dr. Marmer refers to as "release" is at the core of our discussion of the "what" of forgiveness.

Psychologists define this type of forgiveness as a conscious and deliberate decision to release feelings of resentment, anger, or vengeance toward someone who has harmed you, regardless of whether they have earned the right to be forgiven or even deserve your forgiveness. Let's take a deeper look at this core concept.

Forgiveness and Human Nature

First, we need to take a look at and understand a basic human flaw. As stated earlier, forgiving others goes against human nature. When someone has deeply hurt you, they owe you a debt. They have taken from you your sense of happiness and well-being, and you want to take something from them in return. In its simplest terms, forgiveness means giving up our right to get even. In return, you are freed from toxic anger and resentment that trap you in bitterness and hate.

The Biblical story of the prodigal son provides a poignant example of what forgiveness looks like.

Perhaps you are familiar with the story. A father has two sons, the youngest of whom prematurely demands and receives his share of his future inheritance and squanders it on a lifestyle of loose living. When he ends up in living conditions that are worse than the pigs he has been hired to care for, he decides to return home, beg for mercy, and plead with his father to hire him as one of his servants. In the prodigal son's mind, he has forfeited the right to be called a son. The father, of course, overjoyed to see his son again, restores him to full sonship as if nothing had ever happened. In a sense, he offers him release.

As the story unfolds, however, we see the father has actually lost both sons—one to immorality and the other to self-righteousness. The older son is offended that his younger brother has been welcomed home and treated like royalty.

At the conclusion of the parable, we see that the father has forgiven both sons. He restores the prodigal to sonship. He also reminds his other son, who had given into a spirit of self-righteousness and the inability to forgive, of who he is and all he has and will be given by his father. It is the story of two brothers redeemed by their father, not because of what they had done but because they were the sons of a forgiving father who chose to ignore their hurtful actions and chose, instead, to forgive them (see Luke 15:11–31).

To be truthful, as the oldest of five kids growing up, and constantly being reminded to "set the example for your brother and sisters," I resented this parable for many years. I suppose I identified with the oldest son who did everything asked of him. The story left me with a sense that the older brother got cheated out of something. From my shallow perspective, the oldest son did not ask for or squander his dad's money. He stayed and worked the fields by himself. He always did what was right. And he was never even treated to a feast with his friends.

However, over time I learned to view this story through the eyes of the father. As I did, I realized the heart of this story is not the selfishness of the two brothers. It is a story about a gracious, forgiving father. The parable is not concerned with one son getting what he didn't deserve and another son being denied what he thought he deserved. No, it is the story of a father choosing love and forgiveness, notwithstanding the actions and attitudes of his two sons. It is a beautiful picture of the undeserved forgiveness God offers us.

Forgiveness Is a Choice

Forgiveness is first and foremost a choice. Dr. Swartz (whom we met in Chapter 1) suggests, "You are choosing to offer compassion and empathy to the person who wronged you." Forgiveness is not just about saying the words. "It is an active process in which you make a conscious decision to let go of negative feelings whether the person deserves it or not," says Dr. Swartz.[12]

The father in the parable had two choices. He could rest on any negative feelings he would rightfully have had towards his younger son, or he could make the choice to let go of those feelings and forgive his son.

In the same manner, he could just have easily harbored negative feelings towards the older son for challenging his father's right to restore the prodigal to full sonship.

The actions of the father in this story demonstrate that he made a decision to release resentment and anger, choosing to forgive. This is a picture of forgiveness.

---

12   "Forgiveness: Your Health Depends on It." John Hopkins Medicine. https://www.hopkinsmedicine.org/health/wellness-and-prevention/forgiveness-your-health-depends-on-it

As author Gary Chapman explains, "Forgiveness is not a feeling; it is a commitment. It is a choice to show mercy, not to hold the offense up against the offender. Forgiveness is an expression of love."[13]

Forgiveness Makes Things Better

Forgiveness is rooted in a desire to make things better and to experience and express love over hate and resentment. The father in the parable could have easily reminded his younger son of his unforgivable transgression. He also could have reminded his older son just who owned the fields the son was working and who owned the livestock the son wanted for a feast. Instead, he desired to restore both of his sons, and this desire far outweighed any offense generated by either son towards the father.

Forgiveness Must Be Consistent

Inherent in the "what" of forgiveness is the idea of consistency. It certainly would have changed the entire story if the father, after forgiving the youngest son, had responded with anger towards the oldest son's resentment. The father's consistency in extending forgiveness to both of his sons is embodied in the words of Dr. Martin Luther King, Jr., "Forgiveness is not an occasional act; it is a constant attitude."

Understanding What Forgiveness Is Not

Just as important as defining what forgiveness is, we must grasp and understand what forgiveness is not. Experts on the

---

13   Chapman, Gary. *The 5 Languages of Love: The Secret to Love that Lasts.* Northfield Publishing, 2015.

subject of forgiveness universally declare that forgiveness does not mean forgetting, nor does it mean condoning or excusing offenses. It also does not mean you should gloss over or deny the seriousness of the offense committed against you. Although it is possible that forgiveness can lead to restoration of a damaged relationship, the experts declare that forgiving someone does not obligate you to reconcile with the person who harmed you. As much as forgiveness is a choice, reconciliation is also a choice.

Forgiveness provides you, the forgiver, with peace of mind and empowers you to recognize the pain that was suffered without letting that pain define you.

Misconceptions About Forgiveness

Our culture abounds in many misconceptions about forgiveness that can choke out our efforts to engage others from a spirit of forgiveness. It is time to dispel these misconceptions.

Misconception 1: You need to be friendly with the person who hurt you and go back to the old relationship.

Forgiving someone does not require you to trust that person. Forgiveness is a gift that you choose to give to others. Trust must be earned by the other person. You will need to decide whether to continue a relationship with the person you are forgiving or if it would be better to maintain your distance.

Misconception 2: Forgiving someone means having to excuse or ignore what they did.

If you could excuse the behavior of the person who hurt you, forgiveness would not be necessary. When you choose to forgive, you are not excusing them for what they did or what was done. Forgiving them allows you to let go of the bitterness while reminding yourself of your right to demand and set healthy boundaries. You can decide that what was done violated those boundaries and then deal with the situation accordingly.

Misconception 3: To forgive is to forget.

Forgiving others does not eliminate the memory of the offense. Rather, it is the effect of that memory on our well-being that creates the need to forgive. When you forgive someone, you're saying that the memory will no longer fill you with bitterness and hate, and that you have chosen to move on from the circumstances.

Misconception 4: You cannot forgive someone unless you feel like forgiving them.

Many people let their feelings dictate just about everything they do. Forgiving someone is not based on emotions and feelings. It is an act of your will. Forgiveness is a choice you make. It is not a feeling you create.

Misconception 5: Forgiveness means having to become the victim again.

Forgiving is not saying, "What you did was okay, so go ahead and walk all over me." Playing the victim is the worst outcome of having been hurt by someone else. Do not play the martyr role; it only perpetuates the victim mentality and role.

Misconception 6: Forgiveness is a one-and-done event.

It is natural to want to have some kind of emotional catharsis where you forgive and then everything is wonderful. This only happens in movies. Even after you forgive someone, your feelings of hurt, anger, and resentment will arise. Forgiving is a process that takes time. The greater the hurt, the longer the time. Choose forgiveness again and again to reap its benefits.

Understanding what forgiveness is and what it is not will help you understand what is required of you to forgive someone and what that forgiveness means to you. Choose to forgive and set yourself free from the prison of your past.

Next Steps—Forgiveness Is Your Choice

Understanding what forgiveness is and what forgiveness is not lays the foundation for learning to forgive others (and, as we shall see, ourselves) and allowing an attitude of forgiveness to transform our relationships and our lives. The following action steps will help to further your understanding of what forgiveness is and how it has played out (or not) in your life.

1. Take some time to think about and respond to these questions:
a. How have you defined forgiveness in the past?
b. What has forgiveness meant to you?
c. What has forgiveness looked like for you?

2. Determine which of the identified myths about forgiveness you have bought into and ask yourself:
a. How have your false beliefs affected your attitude towards forgiveness?
b. Have these false beliefs affected your ability to forgive?

3. Resolve to eliminate all false beliefs about forgiveness and make the decision to choose to forgive.

Now that we have a deeper understanding of the benefits we receive from choosing to forgive and a picture of what forgiveness should look like for us, it is time to begin the process of forgiving others. This is where the proverbial rubber meets the road—how do we actually forgive?

CHAPTER 4

How Can I Possibly Forgive This?

"Let all bitterness and wrath and anger and clamor and slander be put away from you, along with all malice." – Ephesians 4:31

"Always forgive your enemies; nothing annoys them so much."
– Oscar Wilde

At the age of 14, Rosario Rodriguez was grabbed by a man who dragged her into the nearby woods and began to sexually assault her. Fortunately for Rosario, the man suddenly ceased his attack and fled. Later, she learned from the police that her attacker was a serial rapist-murderer and that she was the only one of his victims to have survived an attack. However, for the next ten years, Rosario suffered from anger, resentment, and severe depression stemming from the attack.

Sharing her story in an interview, she recounts talking with a priest about the sexual violence perpetrated against her. When he encouraged forgiveness, she thought, "But what he did is not okay, and I will never forget it." The priest told her that forgiveness doesn't mean saying something is okay, and it certainly doesn't mean forgetting. Instead, he said, forgiveness means seeing that person as an image bearer of God, impossible as that may seem. Rosario thought about this and states that once she decided to follow her priest's advice to forgive her attacker, she immediately experienced an overwhelming sense of relief and release from her anger and depression.

Incredibly, shortly after that, Rosario was shot point blank in the chest by a young woman during a bungled purse snatching attempt on the streets of Los Angeles. Doctors later told her she should have died on the spot from the severity of the gunshot wound. However, following eight hours of surgery, she was once again the survivor of a violent crime. When her family came from Michigan to visit her in the hospital, her sister asked her whether she was prepared to forgive the woman who had shot her. Rosario said the question actually shocked her.

"It dawned on me that I hadn't even thought about not forgiving this girl, and I hadn't thought about being angry towards her. I actually realized that I didn't want to live in that anger and depression and all that horrible stuff that comes along with not forgiving someone and holding a grudge against them."[14]

Let's be honest. It is one thing to "learn" about forgiveness; it is a new and daunting challenge to put it into practice.

How, for example, did Brooks Douglass find it within himself to face and then forgive the man who had done incredible evil to his family? Or for Robert Rule, who had every right to join the litany of speakers condemning Gary Ridgway, to face the murderer of his daughter and say, "I forgive you, sir." Or for Rosario Rodriguez to survive two

---

14   Rodriguez, Rosario. https://rosariorodriguez.org/

violent attacks and find it in her heart to forgive not just one but both of her attackers?

For us, then, how do we forgive someone who has really hurt us? It is one thing to know we need to forgive. It is an entirely different challenge to begin the process of actively forgiving someone.

The Forgiveness Journey

The forgiveness journey begins and is paved with practical steps. In this chapter, we will walk through these steps.

The journey to forgiveness starts with behavior change. We need to change our behaviors one step at a time to move from a place of deep anger and resentment to releasing ourselves from the self-imposed prison that anger and resentment creates.

In his best-selling book, *Tiny Habits*, author BJ Foggs suggests that successful behavior change comes down to having a plan, and he discusses how we can make behavior change stick. We will take a look at his suggestions for successful behavior change in the context of how to begin the process of adopting a spirit of forgiveness.

The most critical step for successful behavior change, Fogg says, is to create the right mindset. We have to first believe in ourselves and our ability to change. In other words, we must move from seeing ourselves as someone incapable of expressing forgiveness to someone who can choose to express unconditional forgiveness. Fogg suggests, if this seems to be a challenge, it helps to remember when you have accomplished a difficult task in the past and simply remind yourself that you have the ability to do it again.[15]

The second step is to break the desired behavioral change into smaller steps and celebrate each step you take in the right direction. This allows you to avoid being overwhelmed by how far you still need to go. Taking the time to celebrate allows you to acknowledge what you have accomplished and encourages you to keep going.

Finally, Fogg recommends that you surround yourself with a supportive environment. As you begin the journey to forgiveness, enlist the support of others, such as a close friend, a professional counselor, a church leader, or a formal support group. Research shows we are more likely to change our behavior when we engage with others who are supportive of our effort and willing to encourage us through the process. The healing power of community is a well-documented and integral part of successful change.

Steps to Forgiveness

The following summarize the steps we need to take to get started on the road to forgiveness.

Acknowledge What Happened

In his book *Dare to Forgive*, psychiatrist Dr. Ned Hallowell outlines that the first step to forgiveness is to acknowledge what happened and the pain and hurt it has caused you. This could

---

15   Fogg, B.J. *Tiny Habits: The Small Changes that Change Everything.* Houghton Mifflin Harcourt, 2020.

include confiding in someone you trust and being open to expressing how hurt or angry you are because of what happened.[16]

As you go through the process of acknowledging the pain and hurt, don't withdraw or isolate yourself. You want to stay connected and feel the pain, even though it hurts. With someone there to listen, the pain becomes more bearable. Above all else, don't bottle up the pain or try to pretend you don't feel it. Essentially, you want to reflect on and remember the events themselves, how you reacted, how you felt, and how the anger and hurt have affected you.

Dr. Hallowell tells us, you cannot truly forgive unless and until you "come to terms" with how deeply you have been hurt. You need to understand what happened to you when you were wronged and why it hurts so much. One tool to help with this, he suggests, is to buy a notebook and label it your "Anger Journal." In your Anger Journal, write down everything you are angry about, with whom you are angry, and how that anger has affected you. Putting your anger into words like this can help with the process of coming to terms with your anger.

Reflect on What Happened

Once you've had the chance to vent, it is time to reflect on what happened and start appealing to your rational side. Ask questions of yourself such as, "What do you want this pain to turn into? What is holding you back? What is it about the wrong committed against you that is causing you to hold on to your anger and resentment?"

---

16 Hallowell, Edward M. *Dare to Forgive: The Power of Letting Go and Moving On.* Simon & Schuster, 2004.

Consider the simple act of writing the name of the person you have chosen to forgive in your Anger Journal. Try to understand them. Why would they have hurt you in this way? What is in their past that could have caused them to act as they did? Again, this is not excusing their actions, rather, it is helping you see them as a flawed person. Appealing to your rational sense may help you better understand the circumstances in their lives that led them to inflict the harm they did. Dr. Hallowell suggests that you keep in mind that forgiveness is a service to yourself; it is an act of freeing yourself from the poison of hatred.

Dr. Hollowell also suggests that you take inventory of and express gratitude for all that you do have. Focus on your own future and realize that you and your loved ones will be better off once you have rid yourself of anger and vengeful thinking.

It can also help to recall the times in your life where you have been forgiven. Realizing that you have or can be forgiven for everything you have done helps put you in the frame of mind to forgive. Realizing your own need for mercy, grace, and forgiveness enables you to extend the same to others.

Decide to Forgive

If someone hurts you deeply, you may feel the other person deserves to suffer for it. But you are not in control of that. In fact, if you had the power to cause the other person to suffer, you would perpetuate the cycle of suffering, remaining a victim of that cycle, or you might get in trouble with the law.

A word of caution, however; forgiving someone because you think you have to (such as, for example, your religion requires it) is unlikely to bring about healing. Studies have shown that those who forgive out of a sense of obligation or desire to salvage a relationship wind up with a worse relationship. Decide to forgive from your own heart and not because you believe that you are socially or religiously obligated to forgive.

Finally, be mindful that on an emotional level you might not feel ready to forgive. Forgiveness is an affirmative decision you must make on a rational level. You must choose to forgive.

Let Go of Expectations

Recognize that you have no control over how someone responds to your offer of forgiveness. You can only control your decision to choose forgiveness. Once you make that rational decision, seal it with an action, and then move on. Do not make your act of forgiveness contingent upon someone else's response to it.

Renounce Anger

Consider "renouncing your anger" by understanding and acknowledging that your anger can come back, and, when it does, repeat the process to keep moving forward. Keep in mind that going through this process helps you develop critical skills that will make forgiveness less challenging in the future and may enable you to teach the skill of forgiveness to others

Forgive and Move On

It is now time to stop dwelling on what happened. By forgiving someone, you're promising not to bring it up again or to use it against them in the future. You are also promising yourself you will not let the offense hold you in the past any longer. As we observed earlier, forgiveness frees you from the prison of the past and allows you to live in the here and now with hope for the future.

Release your desire to get even (however justified it may seem to you!), and, instead, choose to move on with your life. Consider also how you have grown and changed because of your life experiences. You wish you could have been spared that pain, but it has shaped you and contributed to making you the person you are today. And that person is worthy and lovable.

Next Steps—The Process of Forgiving

Every journey begins with knowing your current location and where you want to go. Without this information, you cannot map out the road ahead, leaving you wandering aimlessly without direction or guidance.

Like any journey, the road to forgiveness requires you to understand your current mindset on forgiveness, including areas in your life that need but lack forgiveness. This is your starting point. This book will serve as your road map for the journey ahead, but the journey begins with knowing your current location and then moving forward one step at a time. The following action steps will get you started on this journey.

1. Identify where you are currently at on the road to forgiveness.
2. Who is one person you can talk to about this? Identify someone to whom you can openly acknowledge the pain and anger you are feeling and who will allow you to vent.
3. From your current point on the road to forgiveness, identify the next step you can take to continue with this journey.
4. Determine if you are prepared to engage in the process of forgiving, and, if not, determine why not and what you can do to better prepare yourself for this journey.

5. Compose a simple prayer or statement announcing your decision to forgive. Something like, "I give up my rights to get even with (insert name) and commit that if these negative feelings come over me again, I will release them. I admit the feelings are real, but I choose not to be controlled by them any longer. I am choosing to set myself free from the prison of unforgiveness."
6. Consider locating and joining a support group in your area for this particular pain or anger.

One last thing to consider. Take the time to realize you are not alone in your suffering. Others have experienced what you are going through. Your personal suffering may be deep and terrible, and unique to you, but others have suffered similar wrongs and hurts. You do not have to go through it alone.

As we continue with this journey to adopting a spirit of forgiveness, we need to explore what many consider to be the "dark side" of forgiveness. By this, they mean a spirit of hidden forgiveness that is hiding in our hearts, deceiving us into believing we are not harboring any anger or resentment that requires forgiveness. "I'm good" does not always mean all is good, and we will shine the light of truth on hidden unforgiveness in the next chapter.

CHAPTER 5

Hidden Unforgiveness—Detecting Unforgiveness Hiding In Your Heart

"Whoever conceals his transgressions will not prosper, but he who confesses and forsakes them will obtain mercy." –
Proverbs 28:13

"Without forgiveness life is governed by ... an endless cycle of resentment and retaliation."
– Roberto Assagioli

At 17, I became a rock and roll bass player. No mystery on why or how. Two of my best friends wanted to start a band; both were far better guitarists than I was. I wanted to be part of the band, so I decided to become a bass player (having no clue what a bass player was or did). This is how most bass players get started!

For the first several months of my rock and roll stardom, I used a rented bass guitar and bass amp (thank you Music Unlimited!). Deciding I wanted my own bass guitar, I took my little brother with me to Don Wehr's Music City, in San Francisco,

California, to buy a bass guitar. I don't know how this purchase escaped my dad's attention. I think we went in the middle of the week, so he wasn't home when we left or when I returned with my brand new 1973 Fender Precision Natural Finish bass (which I am still playing to this day by the way!). And if you are wondering why my little brother went with me, well, let's just say I was extremely shy, and I needed someone to talk to the sales associate for me.

Shortly after that, however, it was time to buy my first bass amp. One Saturday morning as I was getting in the car to head to Leo's Music in Oakland to purchase it, my dad, who knew what I was about to do, decided to position himself in the front yard, next to the driveway, and randomly pull weeds. As I got into the car, he coolly said, without looking up from the weed he was pretending to pull, "Do you really think this is a good way to spend your money?" Now keep in mind, I was spending my own hard-earned money for the amp (as I did for the bass guitar). My father, however, a child of the Depression years, did not believe anyone should waste their money on toys and frivolities. Like music equipment. He refused to look at me when he said, "I am so disappointed in you."

Needless to say, when I returned with my first amp, he did not acknowledge the moment or even look at it. In fact, the only time he ever mentioned this momentous occasion in my young life was when he would yell at me, "Turn that damn thing down or I am throwing it in the trash!" Practice times were thereafter restricted to whenever he wasn't home.

For the longest time, I resented my father's reaction to my decision to buy an amp and his general lack of support for my decision to play in bands (my mother, on the other hand, was incredibly supportive and even got us one of our first gigs, but that is another story).

However, years later, I heard a story that when my father was younger, he wanted to play in the school band. However, the music teacher told him he wasn't good enough to play in the band and that he would never be good enough to be a musician. I have to wonder whether this didn't build up such deep hidden resentment inside of him that eventually made it impossible for him to celebrate or even acknowledge his own son's musical success.

Sadly, my father and I never discussed this or made any attempt to uncover and release either of our hidden resentments.

Unforgiveness can become deep-rooted, leading to resentment, bitterness, and judgmental attitudes towards certain people or situations. The more hidden unforgiveness internally festers in our hearts, the more it can negatively affect our everyday interactions.

As I mentioned in the Introduction, several months before starting this book, the pastor of my church preached about forgiveness. During his sermon, he asked us to consider whether there were any people in our lives we needed to forgive, encouraging us to forgive them. As I listened, I thought to myself, "Nope, I'm good, no one I need to forgive." But then he said something that caught my attention: "Withholding from someone is hidden unforgiveness." He continued emphatically, "If you are withholding your time, affection, or anything else from someone in retaliation for something you feel they have done or owe to you, that is unforgiveness." Ouch!

How many of us, in response to some offense or even mild slight from someone else, engage in the fine art of withholding?

The wife, upset because her husband worked late and missed dinner again, who gives him the cold shoulder and goes to bed without bothering to say good night to him. Or the husband, miffed because his wife has asked him to help with the yard work causing him to miss the football game on television, begrudgingly does the yard work without speaking a word to his wife working alongside him.

How about you? Are there any parts of your heart that are holding on to anger, resentment, or even disappointment that you are lacking the awareness to recognize the need for forgiveness? Make no mistake, that anger and resentment is eating away at you just as viciously as any anger, hurt, or resentment that you are completely aware of. It has the same negative effects as discussed earlier.

Warning Signs of Hidden Unforgiveness

Here are five warning signs to determine if you are holding on to hidden unforgiveness.

Unforgiveness keeps score.

Remember the elder brother in the story of the Prodigal Son? In Luke 15:29, he says to the father, "All these years I've been slaving for you and never disobeyed your orders ... Yet you never gave me even a young goat ... But when this son of yours comes home, you kill the fattened calf for him!" This is what it means to keep score—unforgiveness is always looking at the scoreboard.

Unforgiveness boasts of its own record.

Again, we can look to the older brother in Luke 15:29, "These many years I have never done wrong." An unforgiving spirit says, "I have been good, and others have been bad." But as we have discovered, an unforgiving spirit keeps us from the good God has planned for us.

Unforgiveness complains.

Hidden unforgiveness focuses on what someone is not doing, or not doing to our satisfaction, and says things like, "You never do anything for me." This attitude of constant complaining about some prior offense or failure leaves you trapped in the past. Complaining has never changed anything, so stop doing it.

Workaholics and perfectionists are susceptible to this (and I speak from personal experience). People who don't know how to slow down and enjoy what they have get jealous of people who are enjoying life. If there is someone in particular who aggravates you when you see them having a good time, chances are you have hidden unforgiveness in your heart toward that person.

Unforgiveness alienates, divides, and separates.

Hidden unforgiveness can lead to divisive statements such as a husband referring to his children as "my wife's kids" or saying something to his wife in anger about "your daughter." If there are people in your life you separate yourself from or keep at a distance, this could be a sign that you harbor some hidden unforgiveness towards that person.

Unforgiveness produces jealousy when we are angry at someone who gets blessed.

If your reaction to someone who experiences good fortune is one of jealousy or anger, chances are you need to discover the unforgiveness towards them lurking in your heart and learn to forgive them. Forgiveness is a decision, not a feeling. The Bible reminds us to "bless and do not curse" (Romans 12:14–21). To bless someone rather than curse them, regardless of how you feel about them, is a choice. It is a choice that must be made to begin your healing process.

Additional Signs Of Hidden Unforgiveness

As you consider the question of whether a lack of forgiveness is hiding inside of you, take a look at these additional indicators of hidden unforgiveness to help you uncover and reveal your hidden hurt.

Bursts of Anger

Someone who is struggling with hidden unforgiveness is most likely bottling up their anger, only to have it expressed in bursts of anger from time to time. Sadly, the person at the receiving end of the outburst is often not the person who caused the anger.

One way to combat this is to be mindful when you feel your anger building to the point of an outburst. Carefully consider the source of your anger and be prepared to do an about face when you catch yourself in the middle of an outburst. Especially if the person about to bear the burden of your outburst is not the source of your anger! It is never too late to do an about face. If you cannot stop your outburst, at least apologize to the victim of your outburst!

Petty Behavior

People who are struggling with hidden unforgiveness tend to make snide or petty remarks to or about that person to mask their anger.

When you are dealing with someone that you know you are angry with, take a moment to pause before engaging with the person and ask yourself whether your contemplated interaction with them is going to improve things or just take the edge off of your hurt for a moment. This could be one area of forgiveness you need to work through, following the steps outlined in Chapter 4.

Wanting to Make Sure They Know How You Feel

Often, we operate under a hidden agenda that wants the other person to realize how badly they hurt us so that they will apologize without us ever having to say anything to them about the hurt they caused. Sadly, as previously mentioned, they may never recognize what they've done.

Acceptance and letting go are key aspects of forgiveness. If you are not yet ready to have the "forgiveness conversation," consider writing them a letter that you will never send. Write the letter, then destroy it, letting go of its contents.

Failing to Take Responsibility for Your Feelings

If you constantly blame others for your feelings, then you probably have areas of hidden unforgiveness to uncover and work through. You are effectively saying to the other person, "I hold you responsible for my reaction to what you did."

Unfortunately, this is too often the secret script operating in our hearts. You need to recognize and accept that you cannot control what happens to you. All you can control is your reaction. You are 100% responsible for your reactions and feelings. When you try to project that responsibility onto your offender, you're giving them power over you that they are not entitled to have.

One way to overcome this is to first understand what the secret script is, write it down, then read what you have written out loud. You will quickly recognize how ridiculous it sounds.

Keeping a List and Checking It Twice

If you are keeping a mental or written list of every time others have offended you, this is a good sign that you are harboring hidden unforgiveness. You may think your list is imprisoning them, but it is only keeping you locked in a jail cell while they walk freely about.

Leave the naughty list to Santa. If you have a written list, shred it. If you only have a mental list, write out each item on your mental list. Then shred that list.

Having Strong Negative Feelings … About Yourself

When people are stuck in unforgiveness, particularly unforgiveness they are unaware of, they experience guilt and shame and perform acts of self-sabotage. They are not even aware that the reason they are so hard on themselves is because of withheld or hidden forgiveness.

The way to escape this trap is to practice self-acceptance. Start by recognizing that you are a beloved son or daughter of the Creator of the Universe, and God loves you just as you are.

In fact, He loves you too much to let you stay stuck in a cycle of pain and anger. Ask God to help you let go of the pain and hurt that has been stuck in your heart and simply start loving yourself. And then forgive.

Replaying the Scene Over and Over ... and Over

Do you lie awake in bed at 2 a.m. replaying events that happened weeks, months, or years ago? With each replay, your feelings of resentment grow, compounding your anger and misery.

Sometimes, you fixate so much on the past that you have allowed it to define you and everything you do. For instance, if your heart was broken in a past relationship, you may have consciously decided to let people in only so far, even someone you may have grown to love deeply.

To address this problem, try the following meditation practice:

- Sit quietly where you will not be disturbed for 10–20 minutes.
- Begin noticing your breath and allow yourself to relax for a few minutes.
- Notice all the feelings that are arising within you as you relax.
- Once you've reached a state of deeper relaxation, bring to mind the scene you have been replaying over and over.
- Imagine an ending you would have preferred. For instance, if you regret reacting in anger to an offensive remark, imagine yourself responding to the person and yourself with compassion.
- Imagine yourself in a future encounter with the person or another person. Imagine yourself responding to a similar situation with greater compassion.

- Slowly bring yourself out of meditation.

Choose to be responsive rather than reactive from now on.

Gossiping

It is natural to want to return hurt for hurt.

One of the benign ways we do this is through gossip. We may divulge another's secrets or spread untruths about them behind their back. If you intend to cause harm with your tongue, you would be wise to heed this Proverb:

"Death and life are in the power of the tongue, and those who love it will eat its fruits" (Proverbs 18:21).

When you gossip, you are not only further harming the broken relationship (it's ironic how much you say behind a person's back can get back to them), but you also endanger your relationships with the very people you gossip with. Eventually people will learn that they cannot trust you to hold their confidence, and, sooner rather than later, you will run out of people with whom you can gossip.

When tempted to say something unkind about your offender, try to say something you genuinely admire about them instead. If there is nothing you admire, refrain from speaking about them.

Exercising Poor Judgment

If someone has hurt you significantly, you may engage in unhealthy or risky behavior as a form of self-medication. Think in terms of a cheated lover who engages in a string of unhealthy relationships or a humiliated person who goes on a spending spree. Both situations compensate for their hurt be doing things they would not ordinarily do.

Too often, we justify our risky behavior as a false sense of self-care. While self-care is a hugely important part of letting go of unforgiveness, actions that provide short-term relief at the risk of long-term harm do not constitute valid self-care.

Identify activities you could do instead of engaging in unhealthy or risky behavior and create a list to use every time someone harms you in a way that might trigger such behavior. Things to include on this list are prayer, exercise, listening to music, meditation, healthy eating, breathing exercises, and taking a nap. The key is to create a pre-meditated response to situations that tend to trigger your poor judgement.

Refusing to Confide in Others

We live in a culture that believes reaching out for help is a sign of weakness. In fact, you may be withholding forgiveness because you believe it might cause you to appear weak in the eyes of others.

When you are hurting, it can be helpful to share your feelings with a trusted friend. The idea here is to share your heart, not to gossip about the person who hurt you. When you gossip, you focus on the actions of the offender instead of focusing on your own feelings.

Sharing your feelings with people you trust can free you from the stuck feeling and promote creative thinking to help you move on from the hurt and resentment.

Do not let hidden unforgiveness destroy your life. Identify your past hurts, discover the hidden unforgiveness in your heart, then forgive and move on with your life.

Learning to forgive is a lifelong process. It begins with a daily decision to forgive. It is challenging, but it can be done. Start today.

Next Steps—What's in Your Heart?

As we have learned so far, living with a spirit of unforgiveness can prove detrimental to your physical, mental, and emotional well-being and, in fact, can shorten your life span. However, the devastating consequences of unforgiveness will likely be more pervasive when you are not even aware of the need to forgive or be forgiven. For this reason, it is crucial to take steps now to uncover and reveal hidden unforgiveness lurking within you. After all, you cannot take advantage of the life-transforming power of forgiveness unless you identify all areas of your life where forgiveness is necessary. The following action steps will help you uncover the need to forgive and begin the healing process associated with discovering hidden unforgiveness.

1. Review the signs of hidden unforgiveness and decide which warning signs might apply to you.
2. As you notice the applicable warning signs, take the time to identify the true source of each of your behaviors. There may be more than one person or situation that has caused the deep-seated pain that is holding you back from the freedom that forgiveness provides.
3. Identify actions you can take in lieu of risky behavior as a response to hidden unforgiveness and create a system to implement those actions when needed.

We have now learned why we need to forgive others, what that forgiveness looks like, and how to engage in the transforming healing process of forgiveness. But what if the person you need to forgive is ... yourself?

In the next chapter, we will explore self-forgiveness and why you must forgive yourself in order to transform your life.

CHAPTER 6

Forgive Thyself

"Finally, brothers and sisters, whatever is true, whatever is noble, whatever is right, whatever is pure, whatever is lovely, whatever is admirable—if anything is excellent or praiseworthy—think about such things." – Philippians 4:8

"I think that if God forgives us, we must forgive ourselves. Otherwise, it is almost like setting up ourselves as a higher tribunal than him." – C. S. Lewis

Desmond Tutu, the anti-apartheid and human rights activist, tells a powerful story of the need for self-forgiveness:

"My father said he wanted to talk. I was exhausted. We were halfway home on the pilgrimage we made six times each year. We had driven 10 hours that day to drop the children at their boarding school. Sleep beckoned. We would rest for a few hours before continuing the next day for another 15-hour drive back to our home. I told my father I was tired and had a headache. 'We'll talk tomorrow, in the morning,' I said. We headed to a relative's home a half an hour away. The next morning my niece came to wake us with the news: my father was dead. I was grief stricken. I loved my father very much, and while his temper pained me greatly, there was so much about him that was loving, wise, and witty. And then there was the guilt. With his sudden death, I would never be able to hear what he had wanted to say. Was there some great stone on his heart that he had wanted to remove? Might he have wanted to apologize for the abuse he inflicted on my mother when I was a boy? I will never know. It has taken me many many years to forgive myself for my insensitivity, for not honoring my father one last time with a few moments he wanted to share with me. Honestly, the guilt still stings."[17]

Forgive Yourself as You Forgive Others ... Really

Remember, to choose forgiveness means to make the deliberate decision to let go of anger, resentment, and desires for revenge toward someone who hurt you. The same choice must be made when the someone you need to forgive is yourself.

Ironically, otherwise well-meaning people often find it easier to forgive others than to forgive themselves. We tend to hold ourselves more accountable than we do others. In this chapter, we will explore the idea of self-forgiveness—how to forgive ourselves for something we have done or believe we should have done differently.

First, let's all agree that everyone makes mistakes. It is part of human nature. Elizabeth Gilbert tells us, "There are only two ways to have a peaceful conscience: Never do anything wrong

---

17   Tutu, Desmond. *The Book of Forgiving: The Fourfold Path for Healing Ourselves and Our World.* Harper One, 2014.

or learn self-forgiveness (Pro tip: first way's impossible)."

From time to time, each of us does or says the wrong thing—or we fail to do or say the right thing when called for—and we do it repeatedly. The key, however, is to learn from our mistakes, let them go, and move on. Sound familiar? Yes, self-forgiveness is a close relative of forgiving others. Similar to forgiveness of others, learning to forgive ourselves can improve our physical, mental, and emotional well-being and our relationships with others as well as ourselves. Forgive yourself to live your best life!

How Do You Forgive Yourself?

The first step in self-forgiveness is to recognize and understand that self-forgiveness is not about letting yourself off the hook or excusing your behavior. Nor should you view it as a sign that you are weak. As previously noted, forgiveness does not mean you are condoning or excusing the behavior. This simple truth applies whether the object of your forgiveness is someone else or yourself.

You also need to understand and accept that self-forgiveness and moving forward can be easier said than done. Being able to forgive yourself requires you to accept that forgiveness is a choice. It is a process that expresses "The 4 Rs of Self-Forgiveness:"

- Responsibility
- Remorse
- Restoration
- Renewal

Responsibility—Accept Responsibility for Your Behavior

Before you can forgive yourself, you must first acknowledge the truth of what happened and then assume and accept full responsibility for it. You cannot heal until you are completely honest with yourself, accept responsibility for the mistake, and start learning from what happened.

Facing what you have done is the hardest step. If you have been making excuses, rationalizing, or justifying your actions in order to make them more acceptable to you and others, or if you have been suppressing the action and your emotional response to pretend it never happened, you need to confront this and accept what you have done.

Remorse—Express Remorse for Your Conduct

Once you acknowledge your mistake and take responsibility for it, you will experience a multitude of negative feelings, including guilt and shame. This is completely normal, even healthy. These emotions and feelings can serve as a springboard to positive behavior change.

First, we need to understand the difference between guilt and shame. Guilt implies that you're a good person who did something bad. Shame sees yourself as someone who did something wrong because you are a bad person. The fact that you feel guilty about a wrong you have done does not make you a bad person. Nor are you a bad person because you did something wrong. Express the remorse that your guilt produces, but do not drown in shame.

Repair—Repair the Damage and Restore Trust

One key to move past guilt and remorse is to rectify your mistakes. If called for, the first step might be to apologize. You can also look for opportunities to make it up to whomever you have hurt.

Recognize that while this step may seem as if it only helps the person you have wronged, fixing your mistake also provides an essential benefit for you. It means you can stop wondering and asking yourself whether there is more that you could have done.

Renewal—Self-Forgiveness Leads to Self-Growth

Forgiving yourself will help you to learn from the experience and grow as a person. It will help you understand why you did what you did and give you the opportunity to answer important self-awareness questions such as:

- Why did you respond the way you did?
- Did your response lead to feelings of guilt or shame?
- What steps can you take to prevent the same thing from happening in the future?

You made a mistake, but looking at the mistake as a learning experience can help you make better choices in the future. Learn from your mistakes to become a better person.

Do Not Unfairly Blame Yourself

Self-forgiveness as a model of behavior is not intended for people who unfairly blame themselves for something for which they aren't responsible. Psychologists recognize that people who have suffered abuse, severe trauma, or loss may feel shame and guilt even though they are not responsible for what happened. This problem can be acute in people who suffer from "hindsight bias."[18] Hindsight bias is a feeling that you should have been able to see the hurt coming and avoid the negative outcome.

Self-forgiveness means taking responsibility for your actions and mistakes. It does not mean that you should accept responsibility or feel guilty or ashamed because of what someone else did. You may choose to forgive them, but you should never take on responsibility, guilt, or shame for what they have done.

Additional Thoughts on Self-Forgiveness

One thing that makes self-forgiveness difficult is often when we engage in behavior that is out of alignment with our personal values or self-beliefs, we develop feelings of regret or even self-loathing. In addition, some people are more pre-disposed to rumination, which can lead them to unfairly dwell on negative feelings. This can make the process of self-forgiveness more daunting.

In addition, people who are not ready to change will find it harder to forgive themselves. They will choose to overlook or even excuse the behavior, thus making it difficult, if not impossible, to take the first step towards self-forgiveness.

There is a body of research showing that engaging in self-forgiveness can sometimes reduce empathy for those who have been hurt by our actions. Our inward focus on ourselves required for self-forgiveness can make it more difficult to identify with others we have hurt. Engaging in the active practice of empathy with everyone in your life, not just those who have been affected by your mistake, can reduce this risk.

---

18   https://www.britannica.com/topic/hindsight-bias

CHAPTER 6

What Does God Say About Self-Forgiveness?

The Bible does not specifically address self-forgiveness, but there are many Biblical principles that apply to it.

The basis for forgiving ourselves is the kindness and compassion of God for us in Christ Jesus (see Ephesians 4:32). In Romans 8:1, Paul writes, "All who are in Jesus are freed from condemnation." And in Galatians 5:13, Paul states, "We are freed to love." Indeed, the Bible commands us to display the mercy of God as sinners forgiven of their sins (1 Timothy 1:15–16). Certainly, this would apply to us needing to forgive ourselves of the times we have missed the mark (in other words, sinned).

The Bible also reminds us that when God forgives, He remembers our sin no more (Jeremiah 31:34). This does not mean that God forgets, but that through the act of forgiveness, He chooses not to bring up our sin in a negative way.

In Acts 10:34, we are told that "God shows no partiality." God does not choose to forgive one person and not another. He forgives everyone who believes in Jesus Christ. Applying this truth of an impartial God to yourself means that it is just as important to forgive yourself as it is to forgive others. Forgiving yourself is simply letting go of what you are holding against you so that you can move forward with God.

Paul tells us in Philippians 4:9 that we are to put into practice those things that we have learned from God. If God has moved on from our mistake (as the Bible tells us He has), shouldn't we do the same? In fact, to continue to ruminate and remain mired in our negative self-loathing, shame, and unresolved guilt runs contrary to Paul's admonition in Philippians 4:8 to focus all of our thoughts on whatever is true, noble, right, pure, lovely, admirable, excellent, or praiseworthy.

In Proverbs 16:25, we are told that "There is a way that seems right to a man, but its end is the way of death." It takes an exhausting amount of energy to harbor anger, hatred, and resentment towards ourselves. It is even more exhausting to hide from these feelings and try to pretend the wrongdoing never occurred or that it was not that big of a deal. All of that negative energy robs us of the positive energy we need to become the person God has called us to be.

More often than not, pride lies at the heart of our failure or refusal to forgive ourselves. In effect, the lack of self-forgiveness stems from the fact that, consciously or unconsciously, we have set up a different set of rules or higher standards for ourselves. We are saying to ourselves that we are wiser, more insightful, and more careful than others, and therefore, there is no excuse for our behavior, and it does not deserve to be forgiven. When we reject the forgiveness extended to us by God and refuse to forgive ourselves, what we are doing is setting ourselves above others, and that is pride!

In fact, we are setting ourselves above God! To repeat the above statement made by C.S. Lewis, "I think that if God forgives us, we must forgive ourselves. Otherwise, it is almost like setting up ourselves as a higher tribunal than him." History has repeatedly demonstrated that those who try to set themselves above God have not fared well.

You cannot change what has happened. You cannot restore lives to where they were before the event. You can still make a difference in the lives of others by giving back some of what you have taken. Forgive yourself and let the healing begin.

CHAPTER 6

Next Steps—Discover Self-Forgiveness

Far too often, the most difficult step to take on the forgiveness journey is self-forgiveness. It requires self-awareness, brutal honesty with ourselves and our past actions, and the present accountability associated with acknowledging past mistakes and resolving to do better in the future. Below are some suggestions to help you avoid a lack of self-forgiveness from being the proverbial "elephant in the room.

1. Give yourself permission to accept any feelings triggered by your self-awareness of past mistakes.
2. Fully acknowledge your mistake—preferably aloud—to help free yourself from its self-imposed burden.
3. Consider each mistake a learning experience and remind yourself that you did the best you could with the knowledge you had at the time.
4. Resolve to do better "next time."
5. Move forward using the knowledge gained from the experience to enhance your personal growth in this area of your life.
6. If you made a mistake but have a challenging time putting it out of your mind, give yourself permission to set it aside and return to it when you are ready to proceed.
7. Try journaling to help you better understand your inner critic and develop self-compassion. Write out a "conversation" between you and your inner critic.
8. Pay particular attention to when you are being self-critical and write it down. You might learn what your inner critic is saying is not what you are hearing!

9. Get clear about what you want. If you hurt another person, choose the best course of action to set things right. Do you want to talk to this person and apologize? Is it important to reconcile with them and make amends? It may be easier to forgive yourself if you first make amends.
10. Stop rewinding the tape when you hear "I'm a horrible person" start to play … again and again. Instead, do something positive for yourself, such as go for a walk or listen to music.

Self-forgiveness allows you to let go of the anger, guilt, shame, sadness, or any other feeling you may experience and move on. Once you identify what you're feeling, give it a voice, accept that mistakes are inevitable, then start the healing process by implementing the 4 Rs and one or more of the suggestions outlined in this chapter.

In the next chapter, we will explore a related but altogether different challenge you might face on the forgiveness journey. Perhaps, for you, forgiveness of others and ourselves becomes easier to attain. However, you might struggle with the inability to accept forgiveness when it is offered. This problem has its own set of challenges that we will explore in the next chapter.

CHAPTER 7

Accepting Forgiveness

"Blessed is the one whose transgression is forgiven, whose sin is covered. Blessed is the man against whom the LORD counts no iniquity, and in whose spirit there is no deceit." – Psalm 32:1–2

"Forgiveness is the economy of the heart ... forgiveness saves the expense of anger, the cost of hatred, the waste of spirits."
– Hannah More

In Matthew Chapter 18, Jesus teaches us a parable on forgiveness that speaks to the importance of accepting forgiveness when offered to us.

"Therefore, the kingdom of heaven may be compared to a king who wished to settle accounts with his servants. When he began to settle, one was brought to him who owed him ten thousand talents. And since he could not pay, his master ordered him to be sold, with his wife and children and all that he had, and payment to be made. So, the servant fell on his knees, imploring him, 'Have patience with me, and I will pay you everything.' And out of pity for him, the master of that servant released him and forgave him the debt. But when that same servant went out, he found one of his fellow servants who owed him a hundred denarii and, seizing him, he began to choke him, saying, 'Pay what you owe.' So, his fellow servant fell down and pleaded with him, 'Have patience with me, and I will pay you.' He refused and went and put him in prison until he should pay the debt. When his fellow servants saw what had taken place, they were greatly distressed, and they went and reported to their master all that had taken place. Then his master summoned him and said to him, 'You wicked servant! I forgave you all that debt because you pleaded with me. And should not you have had mercy on your fellow servant, as I had mercy on you?' And in anger his master delivered him to the jailers, until he should pay all his debt" (Matthew 18:23–34).

This story is often used to further the concept that we must forgive others as we have been forgiven. Indeed, in the next verse, Jesus says, "So also my heavenly Father will do to every one of you, if you do not forgive your brother from your heart" (Matthew 18:35).

But there is another facet of this story that shows the pain we cause others and ourselves when we are unable to recognize or accept forgiveness offered to us.

In the story, the first servant pleads for more time to pay his debt, and, much to his surprise, he doesn't get his requested debt extension. Instead, he receives total and complete forgiveness for the entire debt. He was undoubtedly ecstatic to be relieved of his monetary obligation. As the story continues, however, it becomes apparent that he failed to grasp that he had been forgiven or what that meant.

When he leaves the place where forgiveness was extended to him, he immediately encounters someone whom the moral of the story would suggest he should forgive. Someone who owed him a debt that was far less than his forgiven debt. Instead of forgiving his debtor, however, he treats him the way he deserved to be treated by the king. He later suffers the consequences of his failure to grasp the meaning of the forgiveness granted him.

In this man's actions, we see the consequences of being unable to accept forgiveness when extended to us. If the first servant had truly understood that he had been unconditionally forgiven, giving him a fresh start on his life, he would have extended that some forgiveness to his debtor. My guess is he was so overjoyed to be free of that debt that he never stopped to consider the significance of the event. He just knew that was one debt he would never have to pay.

Unfortunately, his lack of understanding and appreciation of his forgiveness cost him dearly as soon as he met the second servant. Because he did not understand nor accept the meaning of the forgiveness given to him, he was incapable of extending it to someone else.

Accepting Forgiveness When Offered

It is a fact that no one is perfect. Yes, that includes you. Throughout your life, you will hurt someone, let them down, or betray their trust. You will create a circumstance that will require someone to forgive you for some failure on your part. The reverse is also quite true— throughout your life others will hurt you and require you to forgive them.

Ironically, accepting forgiveness for something others have done to us is often the more difficult side of the forgiveness equation. Accepting forgiveness for something you have done confronts you with the consequences of your wrongdoing and requires you to acknowledge that you've done something that requires forgiveness. It is difficult to admit, let alone accept, the harm we may have caused others.

Psychologists tell us that learning how to accept forgiveness with a spirit of gratitude and appreciation is an essential part of being a whole, healthy person. Below are steps that you can take to develop a heart of gratitude required to appreciate and accept forgiveness when offered to you.

Acknowledge Your Action

First, acknowledge that you did something that requires forgiveness. Even if you feel you were in the right, do not let your pride stand between you and accepting the offer of forgiveness. In the same vein, do not justify or explain your past actions. Regardless of how you may feel about the situation, from the other person's perspective, you have wronged them. Accept the fact that they feel you have wronged them and appreciate it when they are willing to lay the matter to rest.

Apologize

As difficult as it may be, offer a sincere apology for your behavior. Apologizing does not amount to an admission that you are a bad person. A sincere apology expresses regret. Psychologist Guy Winch in an article published in *Psychology Today*, says that "a genuine apology shows strength of character, can be cathartic," and may cause a restored and even stronger relationship.[19] You don't need to do anything elaborate. Simply say, "I'm sorry that you were hurt. I appreciate your forgiveness." And while it may be tempting to apologize by text or email, do it face-to-face. Advice columnist Slash Coleman says that your apology will be more meaningful if you do it in person.[20] (See Chapter 11 for a more in-depth exploration of how to deliver a sincere apology.)

Forgive Yourself

A key element of learning to accept forgiveness is to forgive yourself for whatever your role in the situation might have been. Accept the fact that you do not always do the right thing. But if you have been forgiven of an offense, extend that same forgiveness to yourself. If they have let it go, shouldn't you be able to do the same?

Make Amends

Making amends for your transgression communicates a sincere desire to learn from the experiences and to avoid a repetition of whatever caused the problem. Making amends may be required to expedite the healing process.

Taking these steps will help you with the challenge of accepting forgiveness. Keep in mind that the more serious your transgression, the harder it had to be for the person you hurt to

---

19   Winch, Guy PhD. "5 Reasons Why Some People Will Never Say Sorry." *Psychology Today,* (29 May 2013). https://www.psychologytoday.com/us/blog/the-squeaky-wheel/201305/5-reasons-why-some-people-will-never-say-sorry
20   Coleman, Slash. "10 Ways to Apologize Appropriately." *Psychology Today,* (13 October 2013). https://www.psychologytoday.com/us/blog/bohemian-love-diaries/201310/10-ways-apologize-appropriately.

extend forgiveness. The fact that they have arrived at a place in their life where they can do so should encourage you to understand the importance of the offer to them. If you can appreciate the importance to them, you should be able to understand the corresponding importance of your acceptance of that offer. Acceptance of forgiveness has as much healing power as offering forgiveness.

Accept God's Forgiveness

Some people—especially people of faith—struggle accepting God's forgiveness. When they sin, or miss the mark, they struggle to believe that God has forgiven them, resulting in a corresponding struggle with accepting God's forgiveness.

Fortunately, there are concrete steps we can take to understand, accept, and experience the power of God's forgiveness in our lives.

The first step is to confess. Tell God what you have done. Yes, He already knows, but as we have learned, forgiveness is impossible if you don't first admit that you did something wrong. Name the sin, don't make excuses for it or try to justify, and simply tell God that you know what you have done is wrong and that you are sorry.

It may be helpful to use scripture in your prayer. Learning scripture related to your situation does two powerful things: (1) it puts you in the mindset of better understanding and acknowledging that your behavior has missed the mark, and (2) it shows your faith in God and the healing power of His forgiveness. Scripture reminds us that, "Faith comes from hearing and hearing comes through the word of Christ" (Romans 10:17). (See Appendix B for additional scripture verses on forgiveness.)

Next, ask God to forgive you! After you have named your wrongful action, acknowledged that you know it was wrong, and expressed sorrow for it, simply ask for forgiveness. It doesn't have to be any fancy Middle Ages oratory. Simply say, "Forgive me."

After you have gone through the above steps, tell God that you believe He has forgiven you. 1 John 1:9 tells us that, "If we confess our sins, he is faithful and just to forgive us our sins and to cleanse us from all unrighteousness." And remember, forgiven sins are forgotten sins. "For I will be merciful to their unrighteousness, and their sins and their lawless deeds I will remember no more" (Hebrews 8:12).

The last step is to repent and strive to keep from repeating the same behavior. Truthfully, you will sin again. But it is important to ask in that moment for God's help to turn away from your wrong behavior. Acts 2:38 tells us to repent, and Jesus warned us to "repent, for the kingdom of God is at hand" (Matthew 4:17). To "repent" means to change your mind or your behavior and start thinking and living the life that God intends you to live. Matthew 5:48 challenges us to become perfect as God is perfect. Recognizing that we will never be perfect, we can make it our goal to become more Christ-like in our thinking and behavior.

Next Steps—Accepting Forgiveness

Admitting you have done something wrong is never easy. It is especially difficult to admit that something you have done has hurt someone else. However, as the unrepentant servant in the Biblical parable learned, the inability to appreciate and accept forgiveness when it is offered to you can have severe consequences. To avoid the negative consequences of living with an inability to accept forgiveness, consider taking the following actions:

1. Review the steps for learning and practicing the art of accepting forgiveness.
2. Be prepared to engage in these steps when you are offered forgiveness.
3. Review how to practice forgiveness so that once you have accepted it, you do not act like the ungrateful servant in Matthew 18 (by all means, don't choke forgiveness out of someone).
4. Ask God for the forgiveness He freely offers, engaging in the Biblical practices of studying the Word, praying, confessing, and repenting. Accept and believe that because He says you are forgiven you are forgiven indeed.
5. Consider finding people who can help you avoid repeated sins (such as an accountability group or partner) and spend time in conversation with other believers who share your commitment to become more Christ-like.

Next, we turn to one of the secret superpowers at the heart of an attitude and spirit of forgiveness. It turns out that John Lennon and Paul McCartney knew what they were talking about!

CHAPTER 8

Love Is All You Need

"Above all, keep loving one another earnestly, since love covers a multitude of sins." – 1 Peter 4:8

"There is no love without forgiveness, and there is no forgiveness without love." – Bryant H. Mcgill

Anne Beiler grew up surrounded by faith and family in the Amish-Mennonite community of Lancaster County, Pennsylvania. She attended traditional Amish school until the 8th grade and eventually met and married Jonas Beiler. Their life as newlyweds and young parents went into a downward spiral following the tragic death of their 19-month-old daughter. Anne, in her mid-20s at the time, quickly descended into darkness and depression, bringing her to the brink of suicide as her marriage fell apart.

At Jonas' suggestion, Anne sought counseling from their pastor, a close family friend. Jonas says that he knew he couldn't help Anne and was hoping that his friend could. Incredibly, as her first meeting with the pastor concluded, Anne's nightmare got worse. The pastor surprised Anne with a long hug and kiss. In her book *Twist of Faith*, Anne describes how after the kiss, this trusted friend told her, "You have needs in your life that cannot be met by Jonas. But I can meet them."

Frightened and confused, Anne knew she could never tell Jonas about this because "he would never believe me." Six years of manipulation and abuse by this pastor-friend propelled Anne into intense levels of pain, blame, and shame, and she wanted to die. Jonas never questioned his friend's loyalty.

When Anne finally broke free, she realized she needed to tell Jonas about it. As Jonas shares, he "stared at the wall after she left ... I found my mind going to some dark places ... my prayer was, 'Oh God, please don't let me see the dawning of another day.'"

The next day, Jonas spoke with a counselor about the situation. As Jonas tells it, that conversation set him on a path of forgiveness that healed him and restored his marriage. The counselor told Jonas, "The only chance you have of saving your marriage is if you will love your wife the way Christ loves you." Jonas credits his deep faith, which allowed him to reach "deeper into my soul than ever before and found God giving me the grace to do things I never thought possible ... it was the only hope I had: discovering how Christ loved me so that I could love my wife in the same way."

Gaining a deeper understanding of God's love for him, Jonas shared that love with Anne, forgiving her with the same forgiveness that Christ proclaimed on the cross. He admits that restoration of their marriage did not happen overnight, and that the pain, discouragement, and insecurities he initially felt still "crop up from time to time." However, he continues, "I made a commitment ... no matter how I felt. I was going to do my best to continue." Even when they were going through the darkest of those dark days, Jonas had a dream to one day introduce his wife as "my best friend, my wife, the mother of all my children, and the grandmother of all my grandchildren." He says, "My dream came true because of Christ's love."

In a "twist" to this story, through the restoration of his relationship with Anne, Jonas developed a vision of offering free counseling services to help others suffering from despair and hopelessness. To support this vision, Anne purchased a soft pretzel concession stand at a local farmers' market. What started as a way to financially support her husband's counseling ministry grew to become Auntie Anne's® pretzels, the world's largest pretzel franchise![21]

What's Love Got to Do With It?

With apologies to Tina Turner, turns out love has everything to do with it!

Love is the cornerstone of forgiveness. Stripped to its core, a spirit of forgiveness is born from a spirit of love. As Jonas and Annie Beiler discovered in the midst of their darkest moments, cultivating a spirit of Christ-like love is essential to successfully navigate the road to forgiveness. Love provides the sustenance required to complete the life-transforming journey of achieving a spirit of forgiveness.

When we speak of the love essential to forgiveness, we are

---

21   Beiler, Anne. *Twist of Faith: The Story of Anne Beiler, Founder of Aunties Anne's Pretzels.* Thomas Nelson, 2010.

not talking about love based on emotion or feeling. Emotional love ebbs and flows depending on how we feel on any given day, and, more often than not, how someone responds to our expressions of love. This is not Hallmark® kind of love.

The love that lays the foundation of forgiveness is a love that flows from the part of us that is able to see everyone as a beloved son or daughter of God. This kind of love says, "I love you, not for who you are or what you have done; I love you because I know God loves you."

Jesus Christ, as the chief cornerstone of love (see Ephesians 2:20), gave us two commands, on which, he says, "Depend all the Law and the Prophets" (Matthew 22:37). We are commanded to: (a) love God with all our heart, soul, and mind, and to (b) love others as we love ourselves (Ibid.).

Summarized, our Creator commands us to:

- Love God
- Love ourselves
- Love others

It is interesting to take note that we are to "love others as we love ourselves." In other words, the act of love begins with loving and accepting ourselves. A lack of forgiveness builds up a wall of anger, shame, and guilt that traps and makes us prisoners of our past. This makes it difficult to love ourselves, challenging to love others, and impossible to love God. Without such love, there can be no forgiveness.

We need to love in order to forgive, and we need to forgive to release love. The release of love allows us to choose and develop a spirit of forgiveness.

As noted, we are commanded to love God. The Bible tells us we demonstrate that love by following the commands of Jesus (see John 14:15). In other words, it is insufficient to simply state that we love God; we are required to show that love through our actions and behavior.

A spirit of anger, resentment, or shame challenges our ability to love God or even say we love God. If we find it challenging to love God because of our anger, we will find it impossible to put love into action and forgive ourselves and others. It becomes a vicious cycle of being unable to love and, therefore, unable to forgive.

The Bible reminds us repeatedly that God is love (see 1 John 4:7). The Bible is also full of reminders that we are commanded to love as God loves us. "We love because he first loved us" (1 John 4:9). But how can we understand and experience God's love and what it looks like?

I heard a sermon that offered an awesome answer to this question. The preacher first shared what many consider the most succinct statement on love ever written:

"Love is patient, love is kind. It does not envy, it does not boast, it is not proud. It does not dishonor others, it is not self-seeking, it is not easily angered, it keeps no record of wrongs. Love does not delight in evil but rejoices with the truth. It always protects, always trusts, always hopes, always perseveres. Love never fails." – 1 Corinthians 13:4–8

Now, substitute the word "God" for each reference to love:

"God is patient, God is kind. God does not envy, God does not boast, God is not proud. God does not dishonor others, God is not self-seeking, God is not easily angered, God keeps no record of wrongs. God does not delight in evil but rejoices with the

truth. God always protects, always trusts, always hopes, always perseveres. God never fails."

This approach to equating the word "God" with the word "love" provides a detailed picture of God's love and what it looks like for us. Since we are called to love others in the same manner and with the same strength that God loves us, we can understand what it means to love others and how to express that love.

Once we understand, as Jonas Beiler did, how much God loves us, we can start to repair the broken relationships with ourselves and with others through the power of forgiveness. This is putting into action the lyrics from chorus of "How He Loves" as performed by David Crowder:

"I don't have time to maintain these regrets

When I think about the way ...

That He loves us

Oh, how He loves us

Oh, how He loves us

Oh, how He loves."[22]

So, how do we love God and others in the context of developing a spirit of forgiveness?

Paul reminds us to "walk in love, as Christ loved us and gave himself up for us" (Ephesians 5:1–2). In 1 Peter 4:8, we are told that, more than anything, we must "keep loving one another earnestly, since love covers a multitude of sins."

Jesus spoke plainly when reminding his followers of the importance of love in every relationship: "By this all people will know that you are my disciples, if you have love for one anoth-

---

22   McMillian, J.M (2005). *How He Loves* (Performed by David Crowder Band).

er" (John 13:35). Jesus also reminds us that love comes from doing what God has already commanded us to do: "If you love me, you will keep my commandments" (John 14:15). Jesus established love as the cornerstone of our relationship with God and with each other, and it is this love that leads to forgiveness.

The Biblical Command "To Forgive"

In Matthew 6:14, Jesus tells us, "If you forgive others their trespasses, your heavenly Father will also forgive you." And in Luke 6:47, Jesus warns, "Judge not, and you will not be judged; condemn not, and you will not be condemned; forgive, and you will be forgiven."

Forgiveness is a Biblical command, and we obey this command when we engage in and practice a spirit of forgiveness. This spirit is rooted in a love that is manifested within us and shared with others.

Do you want a superpower to help you become a forgiving person? Love God, then love yourself, and in so doing, you will grow to love others. Especially others who have hurt you. Learn to see them as God sees them, love them as God loves them, and obey God's command to love others and forgive them. Forgiveness becomes the natural outpouring of love in our lives.

Living in God's love allows us to live free of the fear that envelopes us when we are unable to forgive. We experience this love through daily surrender.

"Surrender your heart to God, turn to him in prayer, and give up your sins—even those you do in secret. Then you won't be ashamed; you will be confident and fearless. Your troubles will go away like water beneath a bridge, and your darkest night

will be brighter than noon. You will rest safe and secure, filled with hope and emptied of worry." – Job 11:13–18

If you don't feel loved by God, you'll struggle to love to others because of fear and a spirit of condemnation that flows from fear: "Where God's love is, there is no fear, because God's perfect love drives out fear" (1 John 4:18).

Remind yourself daily how God thinks about you and not what others might think about you or even what you think about yourself. Here are four things God thinks about you to help with this reminder.

God completely accepts you.

You may have spent much of your life trying to earn acceptance from your parents, peers, those you respect, those you envy, and even total strangers. But you need to realize God has already settled this issue of acceptance (see Titus 3:7).

God unconditionally loves you.

You can't make God stop loving you, because His love isn't based on what you do but on who He is. Isaiah 54:10 reminds us:

*"For the mountains may depart, and the hills be removed, but my steadfast love shall not depart from you, and my covenant of peace shall not be removed, says the L*ORD*, who has compassion on you."*

God completely forgives you.

Because Jesus died on the cross and gave his life as payment for your sins, you are forgiven when you accept God's gift of forgiveness. Romans 8:1 says, "There is no condemnation for those who are in Christ Jesus."

CHAPTER 8

You are valuable to God.

The value of something is created by two things: who owns it and what someone is willing to pay for it. You are a child of God, and the Son of God paid for you with His life (see 1 Corinthians 7:23). That's how valuable you are to God, the Father.

When you remember that you are accepted, loved, forgiven, and valuable to the Creator of the universe, you become better equipped to accept, love, and forgive others.

Eric Hedin, Ph.D., a former professor of physics and astronomy at Ball State University, shares a poignant story of this truth after he was viciously attacked and persecuted for creating a college course that explored whether there were limits to what science could discover. In his book *Cancelled Science: What Some Atheists Don't Want You to See*, Dr. Heigel explains that he created an approved Honors College science course entitled "Boundaries of Science," with the following course description:

"In this course, we will examine the nature of the physical and the living world with the goal of increasing our appreciation of the scope, wonder, and complexity of physical reality. We will also investigate physical reality and the boundaries of science for any hidden wisdom within this reality which may illuminate the central questions of the purpose of our existence and the meaning of life."

Soon thereafter, a militant atheist by the name of Jerry Coyne accused Dr. Hedin of injecting religion into a science course, demanding that the university ban the course. The attack "spilled over to the local press," and the national media took up the charge. The university was threatened with a lawsuit by the Freedom from Religion foundation if the course was not cancelled. Dr. Hedin was personally attacked for creating and teaching the course notwithstanding that the stated purpose of the Honors College was to "promote critical thinking about the societal implications of science and scientific discoveries."

The university responded by forming a commission consisting of mostly non-scientists to investigate the allegations. No member of Dr. Hedin's department was included on this commission, and no one from Ball State ever reached out to Dr. Hedin to discuss what he was teaching in the course. Despite not a single student coming forward to support cancellation of the course, and numerous students supporting Dr. Hedin, Ball State cancelled his course, relying solely on the accusations from Dr. Hedin's outside detractors. Dr. Hedin was also censured by Ball State for failing to adhere to "academic integrity."

The ordeal left Dr. Hedin angry and bitter. Most of his anger was directed to Coyne and other atheists, who were particularly hateful in their attacks on him. He also felt bitterness towards the Ball State administration and some of his colleagues for failing to support him.

In the midst of this bitterness and anger, Dr. Hedin's wife shared a drawing she had been inspired to make. The drawing showed God with his arms held open to a character representing Dr. Hedin's primary accuser, Jerry Coyne, with the words "Come home, son." Dr. Hedin states that seeing the situation from God's perspective in his wife's drawing convicted him that he needed to see his accusers as lost children of God—prodigals if you will—whom God deeply loved and was encouraging to return home to Him. Dr. Hedin confesses that a spirit of forgiveness came over him that allowed him to forgive those who had persecuted him, bringing him a sense of peace that he had been missing throughout the ordeal as well as the ability to move on with his life.

The power of God's love expressed in a simple drawing empowered Dr. Hedin to see beyond his anger and bitterness, allowing him to choose to forgive his tormentors. In one sense, Dr. Hedin himself had returned home to the love of God, transforming his perspective and attitude towards his persecutors. That is the power of forgiveness flowing from the power of God's love.[23]

Or, as Huey Lewis reminds us, "And with a little help from above, you feel the power of love!" [24]

Seeing others as children of God, even lost children, and then loving them because God loves them is life-transforming!

Next Steps—Love, Love, Love

Love God.
Love yourself.
Love others.

Sounds simple, right? But if we are honest, we will admit that love often works better in the movies or a song than in real life. But it doesn't have to be that way. To fully develop and experience the power of love in your life and the crucial role love plays on your journey to becoming a more forgiving (and forgiven) person, here are some key questions to ask yourself. Your honest, self-reflection answers will help unleash the superpower impact of love in your own life and the lives of those around you.

---

[23] Hedin, Eric R. PhD. *Canceled Science: What Some Atheists Don't Want You to See.* Discovery Institute Press, 2021.
[24] Cola, J, Hayes, C, Lewis, H (1985) *Power of Love (Performed by Huey Lewis and the News).*

1. Do you believe God loves you? If not, why not? What steps could you take to better understand God's love for you and accept His love as a gift of His grace?
2. Do you love yourself? Are you self-aware of the feelings you have toward yourself?
3. How can you translate God's love for you and apply that to better love yourself and love others?
4. Think of someone who has hurt you (possibly the person or situation you identified in Chapter 1). Can you see that person as a child of God and loved by God as much as He loves you? If not, what are some next steps you can take to see that person as a beloved son or daughter of God?
5. Understanding love as the cornerstone of forgiveness, what is the next step you can take to release the hurt, anger, and pain you have suffered and extend the healing power of forgiveness toward the person or situation that hurt you?

Now that we have learned that love is a superpower to help us forgive more deeply and meaningfully, you might be wondering, "Are there any other superpowers to help me through this?" I am glad you asked because the answer is, "Yes indeed!" You will have to keep reading to learn the secret of this second superpower.

CHAPTER 9

The Power of Prayer

"Therefore ... pray for one another, that you may be healed. The prayer of a righteous person has great power as it is working." – James 5:16

"When we pray, we are looking for an answer, a solution to a problem or some form of guidance from a power that is stronger and more knowledgeable than ourselves." – Alexander Neal

Russ and Kathy returned home after a ski outing to be met by their son and neighbors. The son slowly approached to tell them their other son, Rick, had been murdered. He explained that Rick ran into the woods after a would-be robber who suddenly turned and shot Rick dead. Russ and Kathy were shocked and could not believe what they were hearing. Their son has been murdered. After hearing the awful news, they went into their home to collect their thoughts and pray. In telling their story, Russ and Kathy share that they felt an immediate peace of mind while praying for the situation, completely dissipating feelings of revenge or harm to their son's murderer.

When the murderer of their son was caught and imprisoned one year later, Russ and Kathy requested the opportunity to visit with him. When they were granted permission to meet with him, they spent time talking with him and they prayed with him. At the end of this meeting, they told him they had forgiven him for taking the life of their son.

I know what you might be thinking as you read this story: "I don't think I could find it in my heart to forgive someone who had murdered a loved one." The same sentiment probably extends to the stories about Brooks Douglass, Robert Rule, Rosario Rodriquez, and Jonas Bieler, who found strength to forgive those who had imposed vile harm on their families.

The truth is you cannot find strength to do this on your own. As the stories shared in this book have unfolded, you can see a common thread. Prayer. Each of them prayed for the ability to forgive.

This is the power of prayer at work. It doesn't matter your religious preference, each of us needs the ability and willingness to call on a power higher than ourselves for wisdom and guidance to travel the road of forgiveness.

It is a fact of life that we all are guilty of doing something that has hurt someone else. Every one of us at one time or another has committed a hurtful act, violated a trust, or otherwise done something that needs to be forgiven.

Here is another fact—the Gallup News Services reports that 9 in 10 Americans claim to engage in prayer, a proportion that has not changed over the last half-century of Gallup polling.[25]

---

25   The Gallup Organization. Washington, D.C.: Gallup Organization, 1999. https://news.gallup.com/poll/3874/nation-observes-national-day-prayer-pray-daily

These two facts led Florida State University psychologist Nathaniel Lambert to develop two experiments to see what would happen if we directed prayer at people who have wronged us. The project sought to determine whether directed prayer might spark forgiveness.

In an article appearing in *Psychological Science*, a journal of the Association for Psychological Science, Lambert describes how he and his colleagues tested this theory using two separate experiments.[26] In the first experiment, they had a group of men and women pray a single prayer for their partner's well-being. The control group merely described their partner by speaking into a tape recorder.

The scientists then sought to measure forgiveness, which they defined as the "diminishing of the initial negative feelings that arise when you've been wronged." The results showed that those who had prayed for their partner harbored fewer vengeful thoughts and emotions and were more ready to forgive and move on than those who merely described their partners.

For the second study, a group of men and women were asked to pray for the same close friend every day for four weeks. The control group was tasked to simply reflect on the relationship, thinking positive thoughts but not praying for their friend. The researchers wondered whether prayer would lead to increased levels of forgiveness towards others.

The two experiments combined showed that the common spiritual practice of prayer, when directed at another person, ex-

---

[26] Lambert NM, Fincham FD, Stillman TF, Graham SM, Beach SR. Motivating change in relationships: Can prayer increase forgiveness? Psychol Sci. 2010 Jan; 21(1):126-32. doi: 10.1177/0956797609355634. Epub 2009 Dec 11. PMID: 20424033.

erted healing effects that increased levels of forgiveness. The researchers theorized that while most of the time people in relationships have shared goals, when they hit a rough patch, they often become adversarial and shift cognitive focus to themselves leading to selfish goals like retribution and resentment. Prayer, the researchers determined, appears to shift cognitive focus back to others, which allows for resentment to recede, and the shared goals once again become the main focus. This, they concluded, leads to forgiveness.[27]

Modern science confirms that the Bible tells us about the power of prayer. In fact, the Bible, from Genesis through Revelation, is a continuing love story between God and people, reflecting both our need for prayer and the power of that prayer. This is perhaps best summarized in James 5:16: "Therefore ... pray for one another, that you may be healed. The prayer of a righteous person has great power as it is working."

In what is referred to as "The Lord's Prayer" (Matthew 6:9–13), Jesus teaches the disciples a model prayer, telling them to, "Pray then like this" (Matthew 6:9). The prayer includes the following words at the heart of our discussion on forgiveness: "[A]nd forgive us our debts, as we have forgiven our debtors" (Matthew 6:12).

As modeled by Jesus throughout His life and ultimately on the cross, forgiving others recognizes, accepts, and embraces God's forgiveness of us. Pastor Jeff Warren of Park Cities Baptist Church in Dallas, Texas puts it like this: "We owed a debt we could not pay, while Jesus paid a debt he did not owe—all so we would forgive as we live forgiven."

---

27   Ibid.

I suggest you start each day with a prayer, asking God to help you become a more forgiving person. Take time to pray for the strength to forgive someone who has personally wronged you. In your prayer, ask God to help you:

- Rediscover the person's humanity
- Surrender your right to get even with the person
- Show them grace and mercy
- Release the person from the hurt they caused you
- Embrace the freedom and healing that comes from a spirit of forgiveness

Or pray something like this (insert the name of the person you are seeking to forgive in the blanks):

"God, I need your help. It seems like such an impossible challenge to forgive _____ and I know I cannot do this on my own. Please be with me each step of this process. I pray for courage to continue on this path to forgiveness. Grant me the wisdom to understand the next step I need to take, and give me the strength to take that next step. Help me to understand how deeply you love me and to find the strength to love _____ as you love them and as you love me. Help me understand that is only in complete forgiveness that I can release myself from the prison of the past and begin living the life you intend for me to live. Thank you."

Next Steps—Use the Power of Prayer

The secret to using the power of prayer to practice forgiveness isn't really that much of a secret. Simply start and cultivate a practice of regular prayer. You do not need any fancy liturgy or special religious words to develop a meaningful prayer practice. Prayer is nothing more than a conversation between you and God, so the words you use should be conversational. Talk to God the way you would talk to a friend, and don't be shy or hesitant in what you say. God wants to hear what is on your heart—the good, the bad, and the ugly. Just say it, He can take it.

The following action steps will help you get started on incorporating regular prayer into your life:

1. Engage in daily prayer directed specifically to the person or situation that has led you to feeling angry or hurt.
2. After a period of time, assess whether directed prayer is moving you toward forgiveness. If so, keep going! If not, reflect on the why, what, and how of forgiveness discussed in this book, determine where you are getting off track, and adjust accordingly.
3. If necessary, modify your prayer to focus on where you are getting off track and where you need help engaging in a specific part of the forgiveness process.

Let's review how far we have come on this journey to understanding the life-transforming power of forgiveness.

We have explored why we need to forgive in terms of what the science says about its benefits and what the Bible commands us to do.

We have learned what forgiveness means, what it looks like, and what it can look like for us.

We have learned how to forgive others and have identified specific actions we can take to transform our lives through the healing power of forgiving others.

CHAPTER 9

We have discussed how important it is to first forgive ourselves.

We have also discovered the importance of adopting an attitude and a spirit that is ready, willing, and able to ask for and accept forgiveness when offered to us.

We now know that developing a Christ-like love for others is a superpower that can lead us to forgiveness and that prayer is fundamental to developing that level of love that leads to forgiveness.

But there is another key topic to explore. We have touched on it throughout the book, but we need to directly deal with it before concluding our discussion of forgiveness. It often serves as the root cause of why we hurt others and why we cannot forgive those who hurt us. The issue is anger. In the next chapter, we will take a deeper dive into the questions, "Why am I always so angry, and what can I do about it?"

CHAPTER 10

The Ugly Truth About Anger

"Refrain from anger and forsake wrath! Fret not yourself; it tends only to evil." – Psalm 37:8

"Speak when you are angry—and you'll make the best speech you'll ever regret." – Laurence J. Peter

There is a wonderful story about a young boy with a terrible temper who is taught a valuable truth about anger. The boy's father, wanting to teach his son a lesson, gave him a bag of nails and told him that every time he lost his temper, he must hammer a nail into their wooden fence.

On the first day of this lesson, the little boy drove 37 nails into the fence. He was really mad that day!

Over the course of the next few weeks, the little boy began to control his temper, so the number of nails hammered into the fence decreased.

It wasn't long before the little boy discovered it was easier to hold his temper than to drive those nails into the fence.

The day finally came when the little boy didn't lose his temper even once, and he was so proud of himself, he couldn't wait to tell his father.

Pleased, his father suggested that he now pull out one nail for each day that he could hold his temper. After several weeks, the day finally came when the young boy could tell his father that all the nails were gone.

Gently, the father took his son by the hand and led him to the fence. "You have done very well, my son," he smiled, "but look at the holes in the fence. The fence will never be the same." The little boy listened carefully as his father continued, "When you say things in anger, they leave permanent scars just like these. And no matter how many times you say you're sorry, the wounds will still be there."

What Is Anger?

According to the *Encyclopedia of Psychology*, anger is an emotion characterized by antagonism toward someone or something you feel has deliberately done you wrong.[28] Anger can be a good thing. It can, for example, provide a means for expressing negative feelings or motivate us to find solutions to problems that anger us.

Excessive anger, however, can cause problems. Increased blood pressure and other physical changes associated with anger make it difficult to think straight and resolve our anger in healthy ways. Unresolved anger that leads to unforgiveness can cause serious harm to your physical, mental, and emotional well-being.

---

28   Kazdin, Alan E. *Encyclopedia of Psychology*. American Psychological Association, 2000.

Most of us understand what anger is and how it can be manifested in our lives. Everyone has experienced anger either in ourselves or in the response of others to us. And those who have suffered from excessive anger have undoubtedly at some point resolved to control their anger with little success.

We already know what anger can do to us and others, particularly as it relates to forgiving others, forgiving ourselves, and accepting forgiveness when offered. But that still leaves us with questions such as, "Why do I get so angry?" and "Why can't I control my anger?" These are questions we will explore in this chapter.

Before we go further, however, I encourage you to seek professional help if you experience extreme anger in yourself or in those around you. It is dangerous and unhealthy. Get help!

The Nature of Anger

Dr. Charles Spielberger, a psychologist who specializes in the study of anger, describes anger "as an emotional state, that varies in intensity from mild irritation to intense fury."[29] Anger is often a secondary emotion that arises from a primary emotion, such as fear or loss. These primary emotions give us a sense of loss of control, which frustrates us and makes us uncomfortable. A sudden shift into anger mode becomes one way we deal with this feeling that we are not in control of our environment.

Like other emotions we may experience, many internal and external events can trigger anger. You could be angry at a specif-

---

[29] Spielberger C.D., Krasner S.S., Solomon E.P. (1988) The Experience, Expression, and Control of Anger. In: Janisse M.P. (eds) Individual Differences, Stress, and Health Psychology.

ic person with whom you have a relationship or complete strangers (such as other drivers on the road or the person in front of you at the grocery store who waits until the check-out person announces the final total before even rummaging through her purse to look for a credit card, which is then declined). You can even direct your anger at an event (such as being stuck in traffic or a canceled flight). Anger can also be caused by worrying or brooding about personal problems. And a traumatic event or situation can trigger anger.

Regardless of the anger trigger, the root of our anger is internal. That is, the anger starts and builds within us before it is outwardly expressed.

Thich Nhat Hanh, the Buddhist monk and Nobel Prize nominee, reminds us that if we look deeply enough, we discover that the root cause (which he refers to as the seed) of anger lies within us. In his book, *Anger: Wisdom for Cooling the Flames*, Thich Nhat Hanh says, "Many other people, confronted with the same situation, would not get angry like you." He continues, "They hear the same words, they see the same situation, and yet they are able to stay calm and not get carried away."[30]

Thich Nhat Hanh believes the problem lies in our failure to take time to discover the root cause of our anger, allowing the anger to become too strong within us. He concludes that because we have not taken steps to manage our anger, "the seed of anger has been watered too often." As a result, the "seed of anger" kills off good seeds within us, such as love and compassion, leaving anger as our dominant go-to emotion.

---

30   Hanh, Thich Nhat. *Anger: Wisdom for Cooling the Flames*. Riverhead Books, 2002.

Instinctively, the human species expresses anger through an aggressive response. Scientists tell us that anger is a natural, adaptive response to threats; it can, for example, inspire us to fight and to defend ourselves when we are attacked. Thus, a certain degree of anger has been and continues to be necessary for human survival.

However, we cannot physically attack every person or thing that irritates us. We have laws, social norms, and common sense that, by design or otherwise, place limits on such behavior (and punish us when our behavior exceeds those limits).

Anger management specialists have identified three methods for expressing anger that, when done correctly, can be healthy and beneficial to you and to others.

First, we can express our angry feelings in an assertive—not aggressive—manner. This is by far the healthiest way to express anger. The challenge is to make clear what your needs are, and how you need them to be met, without hurting others. Healthy assertive anger means being respectful of yourself and others.

Anger can also be converted or redirected. This method involves holding your anger and redirecting your focus to something positive. The aim is to convert your anger into more constructive behavior.

The danger in this approach is that an inability to effectively redirect anger toward something positive can force the anger to turn inward, leading to hypertension, high blood pressure, or depression. Unexpressed anger can lead to pathological responses such as passive-aggressive behavior, putting people down, criticizing everything, and cynical comments. People who engage in these types of behaviors have not learned how to constructively express their anger.

A third healthy method of controlling anger is to calm down inside. This requires you to control your outward behavior and your internal responses, taking steps to calm yourself down until the angry feelings subside.

Dr. Spielberger notes, "When none of these three techniques work, that's when someone—or something—is going to get hurt."[31]

According to Jerry Deffenbacher, Ph.D., an anger management specialist, some people actually get angry more easily and more intensely than others.[32] People who are easily angered have a low tolerance for frustration or a heightened sense of self-entitlement. They feel they should not be subjected to frustration, inconvenience, or annoyance, and they struggle to take things in stride. They are particularly infuriated if the situation seems somehow unjust, and they get to define what is just (like the driver stopped at the red light who doesn't go the millisecond the light turns green).

Why are some people like this? One reason may be genetic or physiological. There are studies suggesting that some children are just born irritable and easily angered. Another cause may be sociocultural. Often, we are taught that it is okay to express anxiety, worry, or other emotions, but that it is not okay to express anger. As a result, we don't learn how to handle or channel anger in a constructive manner.

Research has also found that family background can play a role. Typically, people who are easily angered come from dis-

---

31 Spielberger C.D., Krasner S.S., Solomon E.P. (1988) The Experience, Expression, and Control of Anger. In: Janisse M.P. (eds) Individual Differences, Stress, and Health Psychology.
32 Contributions to Psychology and Medicine. Springer, New York, NY. https://doi.org/10.1007/978-1-4612-3824-9_5

ruptive, chaotic family situations lacking in emotional communication and relationship building skills.

Anger Management

Anger management specialists have identified several useful methods for helping control or at least express anger in a healthy manner. These include:

Relaxation

Relaxation tools, such as deep breathing and relaxing imagery, can help calm down angry feelings. There are books and courses that can teach you relaxation techniques that, once learned, can be used to diffuse your anger in any situation.

Cognitive Restructuring

Cognitive restructuring means to changing the way you think. Angry people tend to react overly dramatically to the simplest thing. Their inner thoughts and exaggerated response are expressed in an angry outburst. Cognitive restructuring teaches us to replace our irrational thoughts with more rational responses. Reminding yourself that something that has triggered your anger might not be to your liking but that it is not "the end of the world" can help in these situations.

Applying Logic to the Situation

Remind yourself that, logically speaking, getting angry will not fix anything. Logic defeats anger, so apply cold hard logic to the situation. Doing this every time you feel anger getting the best of you gives you a better and more balanced perspective.

Problem Solving

Sometimes anger and frustration are caused by very real and inescapable problems in our lives. Unfortunately, modern culture teaches that every problem has a solution. This is simply not true, and it can add to our frustration to find out that there isn't any solution to the problem causing us to be angry. Sometimes, the best "solution" is to focus on how you handle and face the problem.

Improving Communication Skills

Angry people tend to act on assumptions that subsequently prove to be incorrect. Take the time to think through your response, and do not say the first thing that comes into your head. Carefully consider what you want to say. As the saying goes, "Keep your head even if everyone around you is losing theirs."

Using Appropriate Humor

It helps to find the humor in a situation and, in particular, in your response to it. Angry people typically feel, "Everything should go the way I want it to." Try to realize how ridiculous this sounds, and don't take yourself so seriously. Anger is a serious emotion that is often accompanied by thoughts and ideas that, if you take the time to think about them, will make you laugh.

Changing your environment

Sometimes our immediate surroundings cause frustrations that lead to anger. Create personal time for yourself throughout the day where you can minimize the frustrations that can build up over time. A brief pause in your day can help you transition to better handling situations without losing your temper

Seeking Professional Help

If your anger is out of control and negatively impacts you, your relationships, and other important aspects of your life, seek professional help. A qualified mental health professional can help you develop a range of healthy techniques to change thinking and your behavior that results in anger outbursts.

Most days will be filled with frustration, pain, and others acting in ways that are not to your liking. Recognize and accept that you cannot control what others do. You can only control how you respond. Learn and practice anger transforming techniques to help you control your anger.

Anger: From God's Perspective

Throughout the Bible, Scripture warns us of the danger and foolishness of anger. Consider the following verses:

"Whoever is slow to anger has great understanding, but he who has a hasty temper exalts folly" (Proverbs 14:29).

"Make no friendship with a man given to anger, nor go with a wrathful man" (Proverbs 22:24).

"A man of wrath stirs up strife, and one given to anger causes much transgression" (Proverbs 29:22).

"Be not quick in your spirit to become angry, for anger lodges in the heart of fools" (Ecclesiastes 7:9).

"Do not let the sun go down on your anger" (Ephesians 4:26).

"Let all bitterness and wrath and anger and clamor and slander be put away from you, along with all malice" (Ephesians 4:31).

"But now you must put them all away: anger, wrath, malice, slander, and obscene talk from your mouth" (Colossians 3:8).

"I desire then that in every place the men should pray, lifting holy hands without anger or quarreling" (1 Timothy 2:8).

"Let every person be quick to hear, slow to speak, slow to anger" (James 1:19).

(For many years I had the words of James 1:19 as a scrolling screen saver on my work computer to help with my own anger issues ... until the company I worked for took away our right to personalize our screensaver.)

And one last verse to consider, which perhaps best summarizes everything that is wrong with unrighteous anger from God's perspective:

"[F]or the anger of man does not produce the righteousness of God" (James 1:20).

There are two interesting insights or truths we can draw from these scriptural references. The first truth is that anger can serve as the root cause of an inability to forgive. However, anger is also often the root cause of a person's behavior that led to the wrongdoing that needs to be forgiven. The Bible identifies a universal truth confirmed by modern science: Unresolved anger lies at the heart of unforgiveness for the person who gets angry and the person towards whom that anger is cast.

The second truth is that not all anger is bad. This often comes as a shock to otherwise well-meaning believers who claim that anger is a sin. The Bible, however, distinguishes between righteous and unrighteous anger.

Jesus, we are told, was a man without sin (e.g., 1 John 3:5; 2 Corinthians 5:21; and 1 Peter 2:22). Yet the Bible also tells us of the angry response of Jesus when he saw the House of God being used as a marketplace:

"In the temple courts he found people selling cattle, sheep

CHAPTER 10

and doves, and others sitting at tables exchanging money. So, he made a whip out of cords, and drove all from the temple courts, both sheep and cattle; he scattered the coins of the money changers and overturned their tables. To those who sold doves he said, 'Get these out of here! Stop turning my Father's house into a market!'" (John 2:14–16).

Jesus' anger at the merchants and moneychangers undermines any claim that all anger is sin. Jesus got angry, but for the right reasons. His anger, in this case, was triggered by and directed at a situation that dishonored God and took advantage of the people of God. This is righteous anger, and both God and man express righteous anger throughout the Bible.

Compare the righteous anger of Jesus to the unrighteous anger that led to his arrest, persecution, conviction, and crucifixion. The Jewish leaders took action out of jealous desire to protect their privileged status and powerful positions. Their unrighteousness indignation had led them to believe they had exclusive knowledge and domain over the religious beliefs of the Jewish people. They reacted with unrighteous anger at the words and behavior of a commoner from Nazareth who boldly spoke out against them and the carefully constructed rules they relied on to maintain a stranglehold on power.

Also consider the anger of the Romans who carried out the brutal torture and death sentence. They were fearful of what leadership in Rome would do to them if they let the situation continue to get out of hand. This led to unrighteous anger directed towards a Jew who apparently wanted to threaten Roman power and order.

Two very different pictures of anger—the righteous and zealous anger of Jesus and the unrighteous and jealous anger of those who condemned him. Ironically, of course, the venting of this unrighteous anger at Jesus had the very opposite effect than what they intended. What man intended for evil, God intended for good (see Genesis 50:20)!

Next Steps—Control Your Anger

Anger surfaces in so many different, often benign situations and manifests itself in a variety of forms, so it is important to gain a deeper understanding of your anger and to develop methods that work for you to get anger under control. This also applies to the anger of others in your life. In deciding to address the anger in your life and to be able to better respond to the anger of others, consider the following expert-developed suggestions

1. Assess where you or someone else is on an anger scale of 1 to 10. There are tools available to help with this, but you can decide your own scoring. (Presumably, if you are reading this, you are someone who wants to better manage anger in your life, so you already have some idea of what that anger looks like.)
2. If the person scores below a 3 on your anger scale, you can probably work through specific situations by talking it out.
3. If you or they score in the 3 to 6 range, consider implementing one or more of the anger management tools described in this chapter.
4. If you or the other person scores a 7 or higher, consider getting professional help. The anger situation will not get better on its own, and the help and guidance

of a mental health professional to learn, practice, and implement appropriate anger management tools will be immeasurably beneficial.

Above all else, do not let anger ruin your life, and do not let an angry person hurt you. Get help!

We arrive now at the question, "What should we do when our anger has erupted and caused us to act in a harmful way towards others or to say things that are hurtful and mean?" In the next chapter, we will explore what experts have deemed a crucial antidote to misplaced anger (and the hurt it can cause others) and a key step on the road to forgiveness.

CHAPTER 11

How to Apologize ... And Mean It!

"It's hard for me to say I'm sorry, I just want you to know." –
Peter Cetera (1982)

"Pride goes before destruction, and a haughty spirit before a fall." – Proverbs 16:18

a·pol·o·gize
/əˈpäləˌjīz/
verb
gerund or present participle: apologizing
1. express regret for something that one has done wrong.

"I must apologize for disturbing you like this."
Pulitzer Prize-winning journalist, Tom Hallman, Jr., shares a poignant story of the time his third-grade teacher organized a Christmas gift exchange. On the big day, the kids sat in a circle, taking turns ripping open a fancy package that always held some new, shiny toy. Then it was his turn, and his story begins.

"The teacher handed me something that had been wrapped in paper that was clearly reused. It was so wrinkled and re-taped that the colors had faded. With everyone watching, I peeled back the paper and pulled out a cheap paperback book with torn and dirty pages. Tucked inside was a handwritten note identifying the girl who gave it to me. When I announced her name, my classmates started laughing. Her gift was yet another indication of just how different this girl was from the rest of us. She'd arrive late to class, her hair wet and unkempt. She didn't have friends, and the popular students made fun of her because she was poor and wore old clothes.

Even though this incident happened nearly 50 years ago, I remember that afternoon as if it were yesterday. As the class laughed, this eight-year-old girl turned in her chair to hide her tears while the teacher unsuccessfully tried to restore order in a class that had turned on the weakest among us. At that moment, I was worried that the popular kids would think that this girl and I were friends. So, I didn't thank her or even acknowledge the gift. Only decades later did I realize that what I did next was unforgivable: I tossed the book in the garbage."

Hallman shared that for years he has wanted to find the girl and apologize for his actions to no avail. He has never found her to apologize. He notes, "When it comes to apologies, no one gets a pass in this life. Everyone deserves one, and everyone needs to give one."[33]

As Hallman shares this story, I cannot help but feel that the ungrateful actions of the eight-year-old Tommy Hallman and the

---

33 Hallman, Tom, Jr. "A Teacher, a Student, and a 39-year-long Lesson in Forgiveness." The Oregonian: Oregon Live. (22 April 2012). https://www.oregonlive.com/living/2012/04/a_teacher_a_student_and_a_39-y.html

inability to deliver the apology the grown-up Tom Hallman desperately wants to give will haunt Mr. Hallman the rest of his life.

Daniel Pink, in his book *The Power of Regret*, describes a study that asked people, "How often do you look back on your life and wish you had done things differently?" Do you know what people said?

"In all, a whopping 82 percent say that this activity is at least occasionally part of their lives, making Americans far more likely to experience regret than they are to floss their teeth."[34]

The failure to apologize for a wrong action or utterance can lead to a lifetime of regret. Let's dive into apologizing, including what a proper and sincere apology sound like and how and when we should deliver it.

What Is an Apology?

An apology is simply a statement from one person to another that:

1. Expresses a feeling of remorse for a prior action or words
2. Acknowledges the hurt that the actions or words caused

A sincere apology offers benefits for both the person who apologizes and for the person towards whom an apology is made. Apologies help to rebuild broken relationships, especially when your actions or words break a bond of trust.

---

34   Pink, Daniel. *The Power of Regret: How Looking Backward Moves Us Forward.* Riverhead Books, 2022.

Owning up to and acknowledging your mistake with an apology helps initiate a conversation that allows you to take responsibility for your actions and give assurance to the other that you know you messed up and are willing to make amends.

An apology also helps the other person process their own feelings about the situation and accept that they were not at fault and no longer need to blame themselves for what happened.

In addition, the act of apologizing helps us to act better in the future. It can also restore your integrity. Knowing that you made a mistake, acknowledging that mistake to the person you hurt, and resolving not to repeat that mistake ensures that you are less likely to make that mistake again with anyone.

Consequences of Not Apologizing

Someone who is unwilling or unable to apologize admits that they have no interest in restoring the damaged relationship. It could also have consequences beyond the damaged relationship, including loss of respect from others and even damage to your career. Who wants to work with or for a jerk who is unwilling to apologize and take responsibility for their own actions?

If you are in a position of leadership or management, a refusal to apologize can create a toxic work environment. It sets a bad example for the team and creates tension on the team, especially if you owe the apology to someone on your team. Never underestimate the impact a neglected apology can have on team performance! You will only exacerbate the problem when you push the team to perform better when you are the real reason the team is underperforming.

CHAPTER 11

Apologies Can Be Difficult

There are many reasons people find it challenging to apologize. Research suggests that some people don't apologize because of a lack of concern about the other person. Since an apology threatens their own self-image, they choose to preserve their sense of self rather than concern themselves with the impact of their behavior on someone else.

A significant factor underlying the unwillingness or inability to apologize is that the act of apologizing requires courage, and, unfortunately, courage is an absent character trait in our current culture. Apologizing requires you to open up, become vulnerable, admit you were wrong, and as a consequence, expose yourself to attack or blame for what happened. Even when you are willing to admit and accept blame, you might not be prepared for the intensity of the blame thrown your way.

Some otherwise well-meaning people avoid apologizing because they are ashamed or embarrassed by what they did or said. This renders them incapable of facing the person they hurt and openly admitting what they did.

People often refuse to apologize because they do not believe they did anything wrong that would call for an apology. After all, why apologize for something you didn't do? In this situation, it helps to reflect on reasons the other person may feel you owe them an apology. It is conceivable you may not fully understand the impact of your actions and thus are missing something that requires an apology. More importantly, however, whether you owe the other person an apology or not, the act of apologizing can help restore the relationship.

Studies show, however, that the main reason people find

it difficult to apologize is pride. They have too much pride to consider the merits of an apology, whether one is warranted or not. The Book of Proverbs tells us that pridefulness leads to destruction (Proverbs 16:18), and unrepentant pride has destroyed many relationships. As you consider whether to offer an apology, determine whether pride is standing in the way of taking appropriate apologetic action, and if so, humble yourself long enough to offer the apology. Why risk destroying a relationship or yourself in the name of false pride? Get over yourself. It's the right thing to do.

How to Apologize

Knowing how to apologize and how not to apologize are critical to offering a sincere apology. In fact, not knowing how to apologize can make the situation worse.

Most of us have never been taught how to apologize. Think about it. When you were a child, your parents probably instructed you: "Tell your sister you are sorry you hit her" or "Apologize to grandpa for hiding his false teeth." But there was never a lesson on how to properly deliver that apology. We did it under the threat of parental punishment, leading to a half-hearted apology, at best.

As a result, our efforts at apologizing are often vague, lack specificity, and otherwise leave the recipient of the apology doubting our sincerity and feeling worse about the situation. Psychologist Harriet Lerner, author of *Why Won't You Apologize*, states, "When the apology is absent or it's a bad apology, it puts a crack in the very foundation of a relationship and can even end it." This alone, she says, is why it is critical to get it right.[35]

According to Dr. Lerner, a good apology provides an opportunity to take clear and direct responsibility for your wrongdoing without evading, blaming, making excuses, or dredging up offenses from the past. It is correctly delivered if it is steeped in accountability and meets the needs of the present moment. An apology delivered in this manner, she says, can transform relationships.

What makes for a good, sincere, and proper apology?

Psychologists Steven Scher and John Darley suggest a four-step framework for offering a sincere and proper apology:

- Express remorse for your mistake.
- Admit your responsibility.
- Make amends with the aggrieved person.
- Promise that it will not happen again.[36]

Express Remorse

There is probably no better expression of remorse than to simply say, "I'm sorry." In fact, Scher and Darley say that every apology needs to start with two magic words: "I'm sorry" or "I apologize." This should be followed at once with words expressing exactly what you are apologizing for. For example, "I'm sorry I talked to you in a demeaning manner yesterday" expresses remorse and identifies the mistake that you made.

---

35 Lerner, Harriet. Ph.D. *Why Won't You Apologize?: Healing Big Betrayals and Everyday Hurts.* Gallery Books, 2017.
36 Scher, S. and Darley, J. "How Effective Are the Things People Say to Apologize? Effects of the Realization of the Apology Speech Act," Journal of Psycholinguistic Research, Vol. 26, issue 1 (1997).

The words you use in expressing your remorse need to be sincere and authentic. You need to be honest with yourself as to why you are apologizing. If you don't really mean it, don't say it. Never apologize if you are doing so for ulterior motives. An insincere apology expresses neither remorse nor accountability for your mistake. It is better left unsaid.

Admit Your Responsibility

Avoid the temptation to water down an apology with an explanation or justification for your actions. A watered-down apology comes across as making excuses or shifting blame to the other person. For example, saying something like, "I am sorry I snapped at you, but you interrupted me in the middle of doing something important" looks to justify your behavior. This kind of apology suggests you are not responsible for your action or that the other person was responsible for the incident.

Instead, admit responsibility for what you said or did and acknowledge that you were wrong. Without admission of responsibility and acknowledgement of wrongdoing, your apology will ring hollow and potentially do even more damage to the relationship. One can imagine the effect of this conversation on a relationship:

Jim: "I am sorry I snapped at you, but you interrupted me in the middle of doing something important."

Mary: "But you are always doing something important and anytime I want to talk is not important to you."

Jim: "That's not true, but this time you interrupted something that was really important."

Mary: "Then I guess I am not important to you."

Jim: "Here we go again. You try to make everything about

you. Why do you always get so defensive?"

And just like that, the hollow apology leads to the word battle that never ends (and it goes on and on, my friends).

Don't be *this* Jim.

Make Amends

Making amends means making the situation right. Proper amends will depend on the particular situation, but if you carefully examine the action or words that hurt someone, you will discover a meaningful way to make amends. For example, you could say something like, "I am sorry for doubting your ability to lead this project. Here is another project I would like you to take the lead on to demonstrate your skills."

At the very minimum, you could say something like, "If there is anything I can do to make this up to you, please just say so."

As you contemplate how to make proper amends, carefully think it through. Token gestures or meaningless promises will do more harm than good. Too often there is a temptation to offer more than is appropriate, which could lead to unintended consequences or undesirable outcomes. Your offer to make amends needs to be proportionate to the wrong you have committed. For example, coming home late for dinner one night might not call for a trip to Paris as amends, but offering to bring home takeout food for dinner another night would be proportionate. Unless you miss dinner every night; then dinner at a five-star restaurant in Paris might be called for.

Promise It Won't Happen Again

Reassuring the other person that you won't let it happen again is critical to rebuilding trust and restoring the relationship.

Among other things, it shows respect for them and expresses the realization that what you did is so egregious that you would not want them to go through that again. One way to do this effectively is to empower them to hold you accountable and call you out if you do it again.

You must mean and honor this commitment. Otherwise, you have once again proven your lack of trustworthiness and accountability. If you have empowered someone to hold you accountable and call you out when you cross the line, respect and thank them when they do. Never express anger towards someone for doing what you invited them to do in the first place!

A sincere apology communicates genuine understanding, empathy, remorse, and regret, and it includes a promise to learn from and make amends for your mistake. Courage, compassion, and respect for others supply the foundation for a sincere and meaningful apology.

Know When to Apologize

Knowing when to apologize is just as important as knowing how to properly apologize. If you feel or think that something you said or did has hurt someone or caused them to experience hard feelings towards you, apologize and clear the air. It can help to consider whether something you said or did would have bothered you if done to you. If the answer is yes, then an apology must be offered.

If your answer is "probably not" or "I'm not sure," an apology still offers you the chance to "own up" to your mistake and establish boundaries in the relationship. Often, when we come into conflict with someone, we have crossed a boundary in the relationship. It might be an unspoken or poorly defined line, and an apology helps to affirm what kind of future behavior we prefer. This can lead to a sincere discussion with the other person regarding rules you both will adhere to in the future, building trust and leading to further discussion of what you need to build a better relationship.

Apologize for the Right Reasons

A sincere apology makes it easier to move forward and put the conflict behind you.

Sometimes, however, the situation calls for an apology from both individuals. Your courage in going first and apologizing for your part in the conflict may move the other person to apologize for their actions as well. This clears the air for both of you, helping to transform the relationship.

Never apologize just because you expect an apology in return. This is manipulative and usually backfires. In such a case, your apology lacks the sincerity needed for an effective apology.

Never apologize for someone else's part in the conflict. People are often reluctant to apologize first because they think whoever apologizes first is "more wrong" in the conflict. This is false. When you apologize, you are taking responsibility for your actions. That does not mean you are admitting that the entire conflict was your fault. Apologize fairly and sincerely for your role in the conflict, but never accept all the blame if it wasn't entirely your fault. Apologize for what you did and only what you did. It is up to the other person whether they want to accept responsibility and apologize for their role in the conflict. It could go something like this:

Jim: "I'm sorry I snapped at you yesterday. It was wrong and disrespectful, and I will not let it happen again."

Mary: "And I apologize for interrupting you. I should have first asked whether you had a moment to talk and been more respectful of your time. I promise to do better at respecting your time and asking whether it would be a good time to talk."

It is easy to understand how this conversation will result in a much better outcome for Jim and Mary.

The Five Languages of Apology

When we apologize, we tend to use words and mannerisms that would work for us, leaving us bitter when what was intended as a sincere apology is rejected. What went wrong?

In their ground-breaking book, *The Five Languages of Apology*, Dr. Gary Chapman and Jennifer Thomas explain that the problem occurs when we apologize using language that the other person is not receptive to or does not recognize as a sincere apology. They explain that there are, in fact, five languages of apology, and the sincerest apology is delivered in the primary language of the person to whom we are apologizing.[37]

According to Chapman and Thomas, the five languages of apology are:

- Expressing regret
- Accepting responsibility

---

37   Chapman, Gary and Thomas, Jennifer. *The Five Languages of Apology: How to Experience Healing in All Your Relationships*. Northfield Publishing, 2006.

- Making restitution
- Genuine repentance
- Requesting forgiveness

Chapman and Thomas contend for each of us; there is one primary language of apology that is most important and speaks most meaningful to us. While their list of the five languages mirrors the steps to offer a sincere apology, it is the emphasis we place on each of those steps that matters most. For example, you may emphasize accepting responsibility in your apology, but if the other person's primary language of apology is expressing regret, your apology may fall on deaf ears.

To be effective with your apology, you need to figure out which apology language the other person speaks (that is, what is most important to them) and then communicate your apology in their primary language rather than your own.

As we review these five languages, begin the process of understanding the primary language of others and your primary language.

Expressing Regret

For most people, an apology is not sincere unless they hear the words "I'm sorry." The person for whom "expressing regret" is their primary apology language needs to hear loud and clear and early in the apology that you regret the harm you have caused. They feel it more keenly than others and need to hear it emphasized in your apology for the apology to have its intended impact.

Accepting Responsibility

For someone whose primary language of apology is "accepting responsibility" they need to hear your admission of being responsible for the hurt you caused. All of the other elements of an effective apology are necessary, but this is the one element they will zero in on. Unless they hear a clear and unequivocal acceptance of responsibility, they may reject your apology.

Making Restitution

Chapman and Thomas explain that sometimes expressing regret and accepting responsibility are just not good enough for the person looking for an offer to make restitution. Without this, they may view the apology as lacking in sincerity. Sometimes it is something for which we can easily make restitution, such as replacing something we broke or making a child return a toy they stole from a playmate. But sometimes, what we say or do is not easily restored. Chapman and Thomas say that the damage of an angry word or a betrayal can make the person on the receiving end believe that if you truly loved me, you would not have said or done such a hurtful thing. In such cases, making restitution could mean assuring the injured party of your love for them.

Genuine Repentance

If you are apologizing to someone whose primary language is one of repentance, an apology loses its sincerity if delivered with no assurance that you will try not to make the same mistake again. Chapman and Thomas suggest that in addition to telling your loved one you want to change, you need to make and implement a plan of action to ensure the success of your offer of repentance.

CHAPTER 11

Requesting Forgiveness

The fifth and final language of apology can be the hardest part of an apology but may be the most important part of the apology for someone who speaks the language of forgiveness. As noted earlier, asking for forgiveness means relinquishing control and admitting failure. It also means accepting the possibility of rejection. Saying to someone who speaks this language, "Please forgive me," would be the one thing that enables them to accept your apology.

If you are feeling put out that your apology was not accepted or that someone didn't properly apologize to you, the problem is most likely that neither of you was speaking in the other's primary apology language. Take a closer look at these five languages of apology and: (a) identify which of the five languages is your primary language of apology, and (b) for each of the people who are important in your life, whether that be your spouse or significant other, your children, your family, your co-workers, or your close friends, identify their primary language of apology.

Then speak that language.

Final Thoughts on Apologizing

As Luddite as it may sound in today's hyper-connected technological world, the best apologies are delivered in person, face-to-face. According to relationship psychologist Nicole Mc-Cance, it's always better to apologize face-to-face than to say "sorry" in a letter, text, or email.[38] Apologizing in person allows you to express your sincerity with non-verbal cues and allows

---

38   https://www.mindtools.com/pages/article/how-to-apologize.htm

you to read non-verbal cues from the other person.

A written apology may be too formal for certain mistakes and not personal enough for others. If the written apology is not followed by a response, you may be left with an unresolved conflict (and wondering if it was received). At the risk of offending, resorting to a written apology over delivery of an apology in person smacks of cowardice.

It might be helpful to write out your apology before you deliver it. This will give you time to think through and craft your apology so that it covers the basic elements of a proper apology. You can use this to rehearse your apology to feel more comfortable delivering it in person. Just be careful that the apology does not come across as a performance rather than a sincere apology.

Here are some other ways to make an apology that heals rather than causes additional harm.

Drop Your Defenses

Dr. Lerner warns that, "Our automatic set point is to listen defensively," causing us to "listen for what we don't agree with, so we can defend ourselves and correct the facts." She suggests that you, "Try to wrap your brain around the essence of what that hurt party needs you to get."[39]

Be Real

When you are apologizing for something, it's critical to show genuine sorrow and remorse. It feels vulnerable to not be in control of the outcome, but as Lerner states, it is also courageous.

---

39   Lerner, Harriet. Ph.D. *Why Won't You Apologize?: Healing Big Betrayals and Everyday Hurts.* Gallery Books, 2017.

No "Ifs" or "Buts"

A sincere apology does not include any qualifying or "if or but" statements. The word "but" implies rationalization, criticism of the other person, or an excuse. Dr. Lerner warns us that, "It doesn't matter if what you say after the 'but' is true, the 'but' makes your apology false." The person on the receiving end will hear nothing that preceded the "but" and will only hear what follows, rendering your apology useless.

Keep Your Apology Short and Avoid Histrionics

Over-apologizing shifts the focus away from the person who needs to be apologized to and instead makes the apology all about you. Don't hijack the hurt person's emotionality with an over-the-top apology.

Stay Focused

Pay attention to the impact your words are having on the other person rather than your intention in offering the apology. Focus on the needs and response of the other person. Dr. Lerner explains, "It's not the two words 'I'm sorry' that heal the injury. The hurt party wants to know that we really get it, that we validate their feelings and care."[40]

I Thought Love Means Never Having to Say "I'm Sorry"

Perhaps you have heard the catchphrase, "Love means never having to say you're sorry," from the Erich Segal novel *Love*

---

40   Ibid.

Story and popularized by the 1970 film adaption, starring Ali MacGraw and Ryan O›Neal.[41] The line is uttered twice as an expression of endearment.[42]

Of course, as we have discovered, this line is utter nonsense.

In every relationship, there will be multiple times when an apology is not only proper but necessary to save that relationship. In fact, you may have to say "I am sorry" over and over again for a relationship to grow and prosper.

Ironically, the final scene in the 1972 comedy *What's Up, Doc?* includes a conversation between the main characters on this question. Barbra Streisand's character says, "Love means never having to say you're sorry." The other character, played by none other than Ryan O'Neal, responds, "That's the dumbest thing I ever heard."[43]

Next Steps—How to Say "I'm Sorry"

A sincere apology can make all the difference in the world to the person you apologize to and to you. In fact, in an email response to me in April 2022, Tom Hallman confirmed that to this day, he has not been able to locate the young girl he treated so poorly decades ago. He has never been able to experience the joy of offering her a sincere apology, and more than likely, he never will have that opportunity.

Do not let this happen to you. You can learn how to sincerely apologize in a timely and meaningful manner, and the following suggestions can help.

41　Segal, Erich. *Love Story*. Harper & Row (USA), 1970.
42　Hiller, Arthur. *Love Story*. Paramount Pictures, 1970.
43　Bogdanovich, Peter. *What's Up, Doc?* Warner Bros. 1972.

1. Name one person you really care about to whom you owe an apology.
2. Draft a suitable apology that contains each of the elements of the apology framework outlined in this chapter:

- Express remorse for your mistake
- Admit your responsibility
- Make amends with the aggrieved person
- Promise that it will not happen again

3. Make sure that your draft apology does not include any apology killers.
4. Practice the apology out loud several times until you are comfortable saying the words and expressing yourself in a sincere manner. Remember, this is not a performance.
5. Schedule time with the other person. Get the "apology moment" on your calendar. If you have ready access to the person (a spouse, significant other, child, co-worker, friend), you don't have to ask to get on their calendar (that would be awkward). Pick a date and time when you will deliver your apology and put it on your calendar.
6. Deliver the apology.

For Bonus Points:

1. Study the five languages of apology discussed in this chapter.
2. Identify the primary apology language of the person to whom you are apologizing.
3. Tailor your apology to their primary language. Do not

fret if you get this wrong. You can learn from the experience for next time.
4. Determine your own primary language of apology. It may come in handy when someone reading this book decides they need to apologize to you!

We are near the end of our journey on learning why we need to forgive, what forgiveness means, and how to begin forgiving. Our road included a discussion of discovering hidden unforgiveness in our hearts and the importance of learning to forgive ourselves and accept forgiveness from others.

We have also learned the superpowers of forgiveness—love and prayer.

We have explored the root cause of the need for forgiveness, anger, and how to begin healing our anger. And, we learned the importance of a sincere and proper apology, what it looks like, and how to deliver it.

However, before reaching our destination, we need to take a look at some dangerous myths that have been passed down over the years concerning the idea of forgiveness. These myths can obstruct the process for reaping the life-transforming benefits of forgiving others, forgiving ourselves, and accepting forgiveness when it is offered to us. In the next chapter, we will look at ten common myths that need to be discarded to begin the healing process found in forgiveness.

CHAPTER 12

Ten Dangerous Myths

There are many myths about forgiveness that stand in the way of extending true forgiveness to others and to ourselves. Some of these myths have developed over time as cultural norms.

Others find their creation in the murky world of manipulation and control.

Cultural prevalence of these myths prevents those who buy into them from experiencing the life-transforming power of forgiveness. The ten myths presented below are intended for your awareness and to help you avoid getting ensnared in their trap.

1. You just need to forgive and forget.

This all-too-common phrase, offered by otherwise well-meaning people, says to a person struggling with forgiveness that they are the problem. This is unfair. If we forget what happened, we can also lose the learning that comes from the experience. Additionally, sometimes you have to preserve the memory of what happened even if you have forgiven the perpetrator of the wrongdoing. Do you seriously think that Brooks Douglass will ever forget that horrible evening when evil men destroyed his family? Or that Robert Rule will ever forget the death of his teenage daughter at the hands of an evil man who did not care about the life he ended? They are unlikely to ever forget what happened. As shared in their respective stories, they found it within themselves to forgive. But they are under no obligation to forget.

This myth is sometimes buttressed by people who refer to Hebrews 8:12, in which God promises, "I will remember their sins no more." They misunderstand that God's decision to "remember no more" is based not on forgetting our sins; rather, it states His omniscient choice to not hold those sins against us.

I like the way David Stevenson rejects this myth in his funny and insightful book, *Cowboy Wisdom:*

"Forgive your enemies. Just don't forget their names."[44]

2. If I forgive, then it means what happened was acceptable.

As we discovered, there is a false perception that when we forgive someone, it either lets them off the hook or, in some perverse manner, validates what they did. Counter this myth by understanding that we must hold the person who did the wrongdoing accountable for their actions. Forgiving what happened flows from the action but does not excuse the action itself.

3. If I forgive, it might happen to me again.

People who have experienced trauma at the hands of someone often adopt a vigilant stance of self-protection to avoid be-

---

44 Stevenson, David W. *Country Wisdom: What the World Can Learn from the Wit and Wisdom of the West.* Stoecklein Publishing, 2005.

coming a victim again. Sometimes, they are so stringent in their self-protection that they see forgiveness as weakening their vigilance. The cure for this myth is to develop new ways of protection both physically and emotionally to allow the forgiveness process to begin without this fear.

4. In order to forgive, you must reconcile with the person who hurt you.

As we have learned, forgiving someone does not mean you have to resume a relationship with them. Just as forgiveness is a choice, so is your decision whether you want the relationship restored. Think back to the stories shared in this book and ask yourselves whether any of the victims of evil in those stories contemplated reconciliation. The answer is probably a resounding "No."

5. If I don't forgive, that makes me a bad person.

There is a pervasive internal dialogue that tells some of us that being unforgiving makes you a "bad person." Forgiveness is not a "good" versus "bad" person process. It is a personal choice whether to forgive someone.

6. When I forgive, I will never feel angry or hurt about it again.

It is a false understanding of forgiveness to think that just because you have forgiven someone you will never feel angry about it or them again. Several years ago, there was a horrible shooting in an Amish school that killed five young schoolchildren. Incredibly, the day after the shooting, the families of the victims banded together to pray for and forgive the shooter. In a film about the tragedy and subsequent forgiveness, the father of one victim clarified that recollection of the day his daughter was murdered often throws him back into feelings of intense anger and pain, but he works for "forgiveness every day."[45]

7. Forgive the sinner, not the sin.

This myth typically makes the rounds in some Christian circles, but other faiths have a variation on it. To counter this, I would reflect on what Jesus said on the cross: "Father, forgive them, for they know not what they do" (Luke 23:24). With His statement of forgiveness, Jesus asked God to forgive the sinner ("them") and the sin ("what they do"). Jesus rejected this myth, and so must you.

8. Forgiving while still angry or upset is hypocritical.

Hypocrisy would be to refuse to forgive someone because you are still angry or upset at them. In fact, forgiving someone when you are no longer angry or upset is not forgiveness. To grant forgiveness while still hurting is not hypocrisy, it is life-transforming.

9. Just "let it all hang out."

This was a popular theory advocating a "no holds barred, no speed limits" approach to handling anger and forgiveness. Psychologists warn that this is a dangerous myth to the extent this theory serves as a license to hurt others. Research shows that "letting it rip" with anger will probably escalate aggression and does nothing to help resolve the situation. Instead of fostering

---

45   Scharping, Dylan. *Amish Grace*. Lifetime Movie Network, 2010.

forgiveness, the "let it all hang out" philosophy actually makes forgiveness impossible. The better approach would be to discover what triggers your anger and develop coping strategies to deal with those triggers.

10. To err is human, to forgive is divine.

This statement, by English writer Alexander Pope, has led to an argument that only God can forgive people. In his poem, *An Essay on Criticism, Part II*, Pope destroyed this myth by explaining that the statement means while anyone can make a mistake, we should aspire to do as God does and show mercy and forgiveness to them.[46]

If you have ever harbored any of these myths or any other misconceptions about forgiveness, I sincerely hope that this book has served to help you better understand forgiveness. Forgiveness is challenging enough without having it shrouded in mystery, false beliefs, and dangerous misconceptions.

If you think of any other myths about forgiveness or anger, please email them to me! I will include them in a future edition of this book, and if I do (and with your permission), I will give you credit for bringing it to my attention. Thank you!

---

46   Pope, Alexander. *An Essay on Criticism, Part II*. Palala Press, 2016 (originally published 1713).

CONCLUSION

Our journey to discovering the life transforming power of forgiveness concludes with a story shared by a waitress who worked the breakfast shift at a local café.

"This morning one of my regular customers, a really grumpy elderly man who has been eating in our diner every morning for the better part of five years, left me $1,000 in cash for his $7 breakfast. Alongside the cash, he left a small note that read, 'Thank you, Christine. I know I haven't been the brightest smile in your life, and I know we've even exchanged rude remarks a few times over the years, but your smile and generally hospitable service have sincerely given me something to look forward to every morning since my wife passed away. I wanted to say I am sorry and thank you. I'm moving eight hours down the road this afternoon to live with my son and his family. May the rest of your life be magical."[47]

The truth is, we can never know someone's full story.

The guy changing lanes like a madman and cutting you off

---

[47] Chernoff, Angel. "10 Things to Remember Before You Take Things Personally." https://www.marcandangel.com/2021/10/24/10-things-to-remember-before-you-take-things-personally/

on the freeway? You probably could not see the seriously ill child in the back seat he was rushing to get to the hospital in time to save the child's life.

Or the lady in the grocery store line who waits until after her total has been wrung up to look for her credit card? I guess you weren't there last week when her credit card was denied, leaving her in total confusion and embarrassment. She thinks the issue was resolved, but this the first time using the card at the place where she suffered embarrassment last week.

Forgiveness is like a never-ending stream of living water that flows into and out of each of our lives every day. Social psychologists tell us there six components of wellness we can use to identify levels of well-being and happiness in a person's life.[48] Referred to as the "happiness quotient," our personal well-being flows from the sum of our life scores in these six components:

- Emotional
- Physical
- Spiritual
- Intellectual
- Social
- Environmental

As we have explored throughout this book, forgiveness flows through each of these components, and the inability or unwillingness to forgive can negatively impact us in each of these life categories.

---

48   Godbey, Kelly. "Creating Your Ideal Life." Ideal-LIVING Magazine, Vol. 24, No. 1 (Winter 2022).

CONCLUSION

Forgiveness represents the best of what people are capable of as humans and provides balance to something horrible that happened in our lives.

Forgiveness serves as the foundation upon which relational and emotional healing may take place for you and in your life. We should not offer it at the end of the healing process but at its beginning.

Forgiveness is a series of promises to yourself and to your offender that:

- You will not hold the offense against the offender.
- You will not ruminate over the offense in your mind.
- You will not gossip about your offender's wrongdoing.
- You will let go of the offense and move on from the wrongdoing.

Forgiveness cannot be mandated, nor can it be imposed. You must be ready for it and make the conscious decision to choose forgiveness.

Forgiveness means you are ready to express the powerful words of forgiveness spoken by Robert Rule:

"You have made it difficult to live up to what I believe, and that is what God says to do. And that's to forgive. You are forgiven, sir."

Forgiveness can be life-transforming if you allow it to enter your life. Start today, where you are, and begin the process of healing available through the spirit of forgiveness. It will lead to a longer, healthier, and more satisfying life for you and the people you care about.

We conclude with a prayer you might consider praying every

day:

"God, I understand that there is nothing to gain by holding on to unforgiveness of myself or of others, and there is everything to gain by releasing myself from unforgiveness and beginning the healing process of forgiving others and myself. I want to move forward and make a positive difference in the future. Because You have forgiven me, I choose to forgive. I repent of my unforgiving behavior and my attitude of unforgiveness. I ask for Your forgiveness and healing. God, help me to never again hold on to unforgiveness of myself or others. Thank You for loving me and for Your grace to move forward with You."

My prayer is that this book will transform your life. I hope you have learned something useful about the power of forgiveness, that this book has opened your eyes and heart to why you need to forgive, and that this book has given you concrete steps you can take to begin the healing process.

No matter what, I hope you will never hesitate to say "I'm sorry" every time an apology is called for and that your apology will be sincerely delivered.

I am grateful that you took the time to read this book. If you have learned half as much reading it as I have learned while writing it, you are well on your way to experiencing the life-transforming power of forgiveness.

APPENDIX A

41 Inspirational Quotes

"Forgiveness is man's deepest need and highest achievement." – Horace Bushnell

"The more you know yourself, the more you forgive yourself." – Confucius

"Never forget that to forgive yourself is to release trapped energy that could be doing good work in the world." – D. Patrick Miller

"The burden of regret can weigh us down heavily on our spiritual journey. The best way to release regret is to forgive ourselves." – James Van Praagh

"To forgive is to set a prisoner free and realize that prisoner was you." – Lewis B. Smedes

"Holding a grudge doesn't make you strong; it makes you bitter. Forgiving doesn't make you weak; it sets you free." – Dave Willis

"Forgiveness is for yourself because it frees you. It lets you out of that prison you put yourself in." – Louise Hay

"When you initially forgive, it is like letting go of a hot iron. There is initial pain, and the scars will show, but you can start living again." – Stephen Richards

"You forgive yourself for every failure because you are trying to do the right thing. God knows that and you know it. Nobody else may know it." – Maya Angelou

"Forgive yourself first. Release the need to replay a negative situation over and over again in your mind. Don't become a hostage to your past by always reviewing and reliving your mistakes. Don't remind yourself of what should have, could have, or would have been. Release it and let it go. Move on." – Les Brown

"There are only two ways to have a peaceful conscience: Never do anything wrong or learn self-forgiveness (Pro tip: first way's impossible)." – Elizabeth Gilbert

"Do as the heavens have done, forget your evil; With them forgive yourself." – William Shakespeare

"It's toughest to forgive ourselves. So, it's probably best to start with other people. It's almost like peeling an onion. Layer by layer, forgiving others, you really do get to the point where you can forgive yourself." – Patty Duke

"Forgiveness is not an occasional act; it is a constant attitude." – Dr. Martin Luther King Jr.

"In the shadow of my hurt, forgiveness feels like a decision to reward my enemy. But in the shadow of the cross, forgiveness is merely a gift from one undeserving soul to the next." – Andy Stanley

"The simple truth is, we all make mistakes, and we all need forgiveness." – Desmond Tutu

"When we give ourselves self-compassion, we are opening our hearts in a way that can transform our lives." – Kristin Neff

"People can be more forgiving than you can imagine. But you have to forgive yourself. Let go of what's bitter and move on." – Bill Cosby

"To forgive is the highest, most beautiful form of love. In return, you will receive untold peace and happiness." – Robert Muller

"Bring it up, make amends, forgive yourself. It sounds simple, but don't think for a second that it is easy. Getting free from the tyranny of past mistakes can be hard work, but definitely worth the effort. And the payoff is health, wholeness, and inner peace. In other words, you get your life back." – Steve Goodier

"I will permit no man to narrow and degrade my soul by making me hate him." – Booker T. Washington

"Having asked God for forgiveness, accept release, then truly forgive yourself and turn your back definitely on the matter." – Norman Vincent Peale

"Turn down the volume of your negative inner voice and create a nurturing inner voice to take it's place. When you make a mistake, forgive yourself, learn from it, and move on instead of obsessing about it. Equally important, don't allow anyone else to dwell on your mistakes or shortcomings or to expect perfection from you." – Beverly Engel

"There is no love without forgiveness, and there is no forgiveness without love." – Bryant H. Mcgill

"The only true way to create a more loving, productive, and fulfilling life is by forgiving the past." – Iyanla Vanzant

"Everyone makes mistakes. The wise are not people who never make mistakes, but those who forgive themselves and learn from their mistakes." – Ajahn Brahm

"I think that if God forgives us, we must forgive ourselves. Otherwise, it is almost like setting up ourselves as a higher tribunal than him." – C. S. Lewis

"We all make mistakes, don't we? But if you can't forgive yourself, you'll always be an exile in your own life." – Curtis Sittenfeld

"Forgiveness is really a gift to yourself—have the compassion to forgive others, and the courage to forgive yourself." – Mary Anne Radmacher

APPENDIX A

"Forgiving is giving up the hope that it couldn't have been any other way than it actually was." – Oprah Winfrey

"Forgive others, not because they deserve forgiveness, but because you deserve peace." – Mel Robbins

"You will have no peace until you have discovered how to forgive yourself, to forgive other people and let them forgive you." – Dorothy Rowe

"Forgiveness is the economy of the heart ... forgiveness saves the expense of anger, the cost of hatred, the waste of spirits." – Hannah More

"Without forgiveness and love, you will live with resentment, bitterness, malice, and strife, which result in more pain. You can never love without forgiving. Forgiveness deepens your ability to love and frees you from pain." – Kemi Sogunle

"The truth is, unless you let go, unless you forgive yourself, unless you forgive the situation, unless you realize that the situation is over, you cannot move forward." – Dr. Steve Maraboli

"The real difficulty is to overcome how you think about yourself. If we don't have that we never grow, we never learn, and sure as hell we should never teach." – Maya Angelou

"In order to heal, we must first forgive ... and sometimes the person we must forgive is ourselves." – Mila Bron

"It is such a great moment of liberation when you learn to forgive yourself, let the burden go, and walk out into a new path of promise and possibility." – John O'Donohue

"Feeling compassion for ourselves in no way releases us from responsibility for our actions. Rather, it releases us from the self-hatred that prevents us from responding to our life with clarity and balance." – Tara Brach

"Without forgiveness life is governed by ... an endless cycle of resentment and retaliation." – Roberto Assagioli

"Today I decided to forgive you. Not because you apologized, or because you acknowledged the pain that you caused me, but because my soul deserves peace." – Najwa Zebian (Note: Thank you to Tiffany Ashley for sharing this quote with me.)

APPENDIX B

Key Scripture Verses on Forgiveness

Below you will find verses from the Old Testament and the New Testament concerning forgiveness. The cited scriptures deal with both God's forgiveness of us and our command to forgive others.

I suggest the following approach to using these verses on you journey to adopting a spirit of forgiveness.

1. Read through all the verses.
2. After you have read through all of them, choose one.
3. Read that verse to yourself and aloud.
4. Meditate on the verse, its meaning to you, and its application to your life.
5. Journal your thoughts on the chosen verse.
6. Memorize the verse.

Approaching scripture on forgiveness in this manner will help to further your understanding of the nature of forgiveness and to internalize it so that your focus becomes not what was done to you but your need to forgive others.

And if you are struggling with self-forgiveness, my hope is that these Bible verses will open your eyes to the Truth that God loves you, God has forgiven you, and you need to forgive yourself in response to God's love and forgiveness.

I can't possibly know what you are going through, but if you are struggling with your faith in your particular circumstances, I encourage you to "fix your eyes on Jesus, the author and perfecter of our faith" (Hebrews 12:2) and to call upon the truth found in Romans 10:17: "Faith comes from hearing and hearing through the word of Christ." My hope is that by focusing on what Jesus has done for you, and by reading the verses below, you will find your faith restored and renewed for the journey to reclaim and redeem the spirit of forgiveness we have been called to live.

1 John 1:9
"If we confess our sins, he is faithful and just to forgive us our sins and to cleanse us from all unrighteousness."

Ephesians 1:7
"In him we have redemption through his blood, the forgiveness of our trespasses, according to the riches of his grace."

Colossians 3:13
"Bearing with one another and, if one has a complaint against another, forgiving each other; as the Lord has forgiven you, so you also must forgive."

Ephesians 4:32
"Be kind to one another, tenderhearted, forgiving one another, as God in Christ forgave you."

Matthew 6:14–15
"For if you forgive others their trespasses, your heavenly Father will also forgive you, but if you do not forgive others their trespasses, neither will your Father forgive your trespasses."

Mark 11:25
"And whenever you stand praying, forgive, if you have anything against anyone, so that your Father also who is in heaven may forgive you your trespasses."

Luke 6:37
"Judge not, and you will not be judged; condemn not, and you will not be condemned; forgive, and you will be forgiven."

Matthew 18:21–22

"Then Peter came up and said to him, 'Lord, how often will my brother sin against me, and I forgive him? As many as seven times?' Jesus said to him, 'I do not say to you seven times, but seventy times seven.'"

Isaiah 55:7

"Let the wicked forsake his way, and the unrighteous man his thoughts; let him return to the Lord, that he may have compassion on him, and to our God, for he will abundantly pardon."

Daniel 9:9

"To the Lord our God belong mercy and forgiveness, for we have rebelled against him."

Acts 2:38

"And Peter said to them, 'Repent and be baptized every one of you in the name of Jesus Christ for the forgiveness of your sins, and you will receive the gift of the Holy Spirit.'"

Matthew 6:12

"And forgive us our debts, as we also have forgiven our debtors."

Acts 3:19

"Repent therefore, and turn again, that your sins may be blotted out."

Luke 23:34

"And Jesus said, 'Father, forgive them, for they know not what they do.'"

Romans 3:23
"For all have sinned and fall short of the glory of God."

Matthew 6:14
"For if you forgive others their trespasses, your heavenly Father will also forgive you."

Luke 17:3–4
"Pay attention to yourselves! If your brother sins, rebuke him, and if he repents, forgive him, and if he sins against you seven times in the day, and turns to you seven times, saying, 'I repent,' you must forgive him."

Colossians 1:13–14
"He has delivered us from the domain of darkness and transferred us to the kingdom of his beloved Son, in whom we have redemption, the forgiveness of sins."

Psalm 103:12
"As far as the east is from the west, so far does he remove our transgressions from us."

Matthew 26:28
"For this is my blood of the covenant, which is poured out for many for the forgiveness of sins."

John 3:16
"For God so loved the world, that he gave his only Son, that whoever believes in him should not perish but have eternal life."

Proverbs 17:9

"Whoever covers an offense seeks love, but he who repeats a matter separates close friends."

Hebrews 10:17

"Then he adds, 'I will remember their sins and their lawless deeds no more.'"

Psalm 86:5

"For you, O Lord, are good and forgiving, abounding in steadfast love to all who call upon you."

Ephesians 4:31–32

"Let all bitterness and wrath and anger and clamor and slander be put away from you, along with all malice. Be kind to one another, tenderhearted, forgiving one another, as God in Christ forgave you."

Psalm 32:5

"I acknowledged my sin to you, and I did not cover my iniquity; I said, 'I will confess my transgressions to the Lord,' and you forgave the iniquity of my sin. Selah."

2 Chronicles 7:14

"If my people who are called by my name humble themselves, and pray and seek my face and turn from their wicked ways, then I will hear from heaven and will forgive their sin and heal their land."

Acts 10:43

"To him all the prophets bear witness that everyone who believes in him receives forgiveness of sins through his name."

Hebrews 8:12

"For I will be merciful toward their iniquities, and I will remember their sins no more."

Micah 7:18–19

"Who is a God like you, pardoning iniquity and passing over transgression for the remnant of his inheritance? He does not retain his anger forever, because he delights in steadfast love. He will again have compassion on us; he will tread our iniquities underfoot. You will cast all our sins into the depths of the sea."

Matthew 5:23–24

"So if you are offering your gift at the altar and there remember that your brother has something against you, leave your gift there before the altar and go. First be reconciled to your brother, and then come and offer your gift."

Isaiah 43:25

"I, I am he who blots out your transgressions for my own sake, and I will not remember your sins."

Matthew 6:15

"But if you do not forgive others their trespasses, neither will your Father forgive your trespasses."

Proverbs 10:12

"Hatred stirs up strife, but love covers all offenses."

Proverbs 28:13

"Whoever conceals his transgressions will not prosper, but he who confesses and forsakes them will obtain mercy."

Ephesians 2:8–9

"For by grace you have been saved through faith. And this is not your own doing; it is the gift of God, not a result of works, so that no one may boast."

Isaiah 43:25–26

"I, I am he who blots out your transgressions for my own sake, and I will not remember your sins. Put me in remembrance; let us argue together; set forth your case, that you may be proved right."

Psalm 130:4

"But with you there is forgiveness, that you may be feared."

Ephesians 2:1–22

"And you were dead in the trespasses and sins in which you once walked, following the course of this world, following the prince of the power of the air, the spirit that is now at work in the sons of disobedience—among whom we all once lived in the passions of our flesh, carrying out the desires of the body and the mind, and were by nature children of wrath, like the rest of mankind. But God, being rich in mercy, because of the great love with which he loved us, even when we were dead in our trespasses, made us alive together with Christ—by grace you have been saved …"

James 5:16

"Therefore, confess your sins to one another and pray for one another, that you may be healed. The prayer of a righteous person has great power as it is working."

1 John 2:12

"I am writing to you, little children, because your sins are forgiven for his name's sake."

Micah 7:18

"Who is a God like you, pardoning iniquity and passing over transgression for the remnant of his inheritance? He does not retain his anger forever, because he delights in steadfast love."

Romans 6:23

"For the wages of sin is death, but the free gift of God is eternal life in Christ Jesus our Lord."

Luke 23:33–34

"And when they came to the place that is called The Skull, there they crucified him, and the criminals, one on his right and one on his left. And Jesus said, 'Father, forgive them, for they know not what they do.'"

Colossians 1:14

"In whom we have redemption, the forgiveness of sins."

Romans 5:8

"But God shows his love for us in that while we were still sinners, Christ died for us."

1 Peter 4:8

"Above all, keep loving one another earnestly, since love covers a multitude of sins."

Matthew 5:44

"But I say to you, Love your enemies and pray for those who persecute you."

Romans 12:20

"To the contrary, 'if your enemy is hungry, feed him; if he is thirsty, give him something to drink; for by so doing you will heap burning coals on his head.'"

Matthew 6:12–15

"And forgive us our debts, as we also have forgiven our debtors. And lead us not into temptation, but deliver us from evil. For if you forgive others their trespasses, your heavenly Father will also forgive you, but if you do not forgive others their trespasses, neither will your Father forgive your trespasses."

James 5:15

"And the prayer of faith will save the one who is sick, and the Lord will raise him up. And if he has committed sins, he will be forgiven."

John 3:16–17

"For God so loved the world, that he gave his only Son, that whoever believes in him should not perish but have eternal life. For God did not send his Son into the world to condemn the world, but in order that the world might be saved through him."

Colossians 2:13

"And you, who were dead in your trespasses and the uncircumcision of your flesh, God made alive together with him, having forgiven us all our trespasses."

Acts 13:38

"Let it be known to you therefore, brothers, that through this man forgiveness of sins is proclaimed to you."

Acts 7:59–60

"And as they were stoning Stephen, he called out, 'Lord Jesus, receive my spirit.' And falling to his knees he cried out with a loud voice, 'Lord, do not hold this sin against them.' And when he had said this, he fell asleep."

Luke 24:47

"And that repentance and forgiveness of sins should be proclaimed in his name to all nations, beginning from Jerusalem."

Jeremiah 31:34

"And no longer shall each one teach his neighbor and each his brother, saying, 'Know the LORD,' for they shall all know me, from the least of them to the greatest, declares the LORD. For I will forgive their iniquity, and I will remember their sin no more."

Luke 17:3

"Pay attention to yourselves! If your brother sins, rebuke him, and if he repents, forgive him."

2 Chronicles 30:9

"For if you return to the LORD, your brothers and your children will find compassion with their captors and return to this land. For the LORD your God is gracious and merciful and will not turn away his face from you, if you return to him."

Colossians 3:12–13

"Put on then, as God's chosen ones, holy and beloved, compassionate hearts, kindness, humility, meekness, and patience, bearing with one another and, if one has a complaint against another, forgiving each other; as the Lord has forgiven you, so you also must forgive."

Acts 13:38–39

"Let it be known to you therefore, brothers, that through this man forgiveness of sins is proclaimed to you, and by him everyone who believes is freed from everything from which you could not be freed by the law of Moses."

Luke 11:4

"And forgive us our sins, for we ourselves forgive everyone who is indebted to us."

2 Corinthians 2:5–8

"Now if anyone has caused pain, he has caused it not to me, but in some measure—not to put it too severely—to all of you.

For such a one, this punishment by the majority is enough, so you should rather turn to forgive and comfort him, or he may be overwhelmed by excessive sorrow. So I beg you to reaffirm your love for him."

Psalm 32:1–2

"Blessed is the one whose transgression is forgiven, whose sin is covered. Blessed is the man against whom the Lord counts no iniquity, and in whose spirit there is no deceit."

Psalm 79:9

"Help us, O God of our salvation, for the glory of your name; deliver us, and atone for our sins, for your name's sake!"

1 Corinthians 13:4–7

"Love is patient and kind; love does not envy or boast; it is not arrogant or rude. It does not insist on its own way; it is not irritable or resentful; it does not rejoice at wrongdoing, but rejoices with the truth. Love bears all things, believes all things, hopes all things, endures all things."

Hebrews 4:16

"Let us then with confidence draw near to the throne of grace, that we may receive mercy and find grace to help in time of need."

Matthew 18:21

"Then Peter came up and said to him, 'Lord, how often will my brother sin against me, and I forgive him? As many as seven times?'"

Psalm 103:10–14

"He does not deal with us according to our sins, nor repay us according to our iniquities. For as high as the heavens are above the earth, so great is his steadfast love toward those who fear him; as far as the east is from the west, so far does he remove our transgressions from us. As a father shows compassion to his children, so the LORD shows compassion to those who fear him. For he knows our frame; he remembers that we are dust."

Matthew 18:23–35

"Therefore the kingdom of heaven may be compared to a king who wished to settle accounts with his servants. When he began to settle, one was brought to him who owed him ten thousand talents. And since he could not pay, his master ordered him to be sold, with his wife and children and all that he had, and payment to be made. So the servant fell on his knees, imploring him, 'Have patience with me, and I will pay you everything.' And out of pity for him, the master of that servant released him and forgave him the debt …"

Luke 17:4

"And if he sins against you seven times in the day, and turns to you seven times, saying, 'I repent,' you must forgive him."

Isaiah 53:5

"But he was wounded for our transgressions; he was crushed for our iniquities; upon him was the chastisement that brought us peace, and with his stripes we are healed."

John 20:22–23

"And when he had said this, he breathed on them and said to them, 'Receive the Holy Spirit. If you forgive the sins of any, they are forgiven them; if you withhold forgiveness from any, it is withheld.'"

Jeremiah 3:12

"Go, and proclaim these words toward the north, and say, 'Return, faithless Israel, declares the LORD. I will not look on you in anger, for I am merciful, declares the LORD; I will not be angry forever.'"

Acts 8:22

"Repent, therefore, of this wickedness of yours, and pray to the Lord that, if possible, the intent of your heart may be forgiven you."

Numbers 14:19–21

"'Please pardon the iniquity of this people, according to the greatness of your steadfast love, just as you have forgiven this people, from Egypt until now.' Then the LORD said, 'I have pardoned, according to your word. But truly, as I live, and as all the earth shall be filled with the glory of the LORD.'"

Colossians 2:13–14

"And you, who were dead in your trespasses and the uncircumcision of your flesh, God made alive together with him, having forgiven us all our trespasses, by canceling the record of debt that stood against us with its legal demands. This he set aside, nailing it to the cross."

Luke 7:47–48
"'Therefore I tell you, her sins, which are many, are forgiven—for she loved much. But he who is forgiven little, loves little.' And he said to her, 'Your sins are forgiven.'"

REFERENCES

Chapter 1

Smith, Tim. "Brooks Douglass: Strength to Forgive." CBN.com. https://www1.cbn.com/700club/brooks-douglass-strength-forgive

"Forgiveness: Your Health Depends on It. John Hopkins Medicine. https://www.hopkinsmedicine.org/health/wellness-and-prevention/forgiveness-your-health-depends-on-it

Worthington, Everett, L. Jr. "The New Science of Forgiveness." Greater Good Magazine (1 September 2004). https://greatergood.berkeley.edu/article/item/the_new_science_of_forgiveness

Toussaint, L.L., Owen, A.D. & Cheadle, A. Forgive to Live: Forgiveness, Health, and Longevity. *J Behav Med* **35,** 375–386 (2012). https://doi.org/10.1007/s10865-011-9362-4

Cozolino, Louis J. *Timeless: Nature's Formula for Health and Longevity*. W.W. Norton & Company, 2018.

Akhtar, S., Dolan, A. & Barlow, J. Understanding the Relationship Between State Forgiveness and Psychological Wellbeing: A Qualitative Study. *J Relig Health* **56**, 450–463 (2017). https://doi.org/10.1007/s10943-016-0188-9

Whitbourne, Susan Krauss, PhD. "Live Longer by Practicing Forgiveness." (1 January 2013). https://www.psychologytoday.com/us/blog/fulfillment-any-age/201301/live-longer-practicing-forgiveness.

Chapter 2

"Serial Killer Cries Over Father's Forgiveness." (5 October 2012). https://www.youtube.com/watch?v=iY8iWJ5h5aM

Smith, Judah. *How's Your Soul: Why Everything that Matters Starts with the Inside You.* Nelson Books, 2016.

Dillow, Linda. *Calm My Anxious Heart: A Woman's Guide to Finding Contentment.* NavPress, 2007.

Chapter 3

Marmer, Stephen Dr. M.D. (05 May 2014): https://www.prageru.com/video/forgiveness

Forgiveness: Your Health Depends on It. John Hopkins Medicine. https://www.hopkinsmedicine.org/health/wellness-and-prevention/forgiveness-your-health-depends-on-it

Chapman, Gary. *The 5 Languages of Love: The Secret to Love that Lasts.* Northfield Publishing, 2015.

Chapter 4

Rodriguez, Rosario. https://rosariorodriguez.org/

Fogg, B.J. *Tiny Habits: The Small Changes that Change Everything.* Houghton Mifflin Harcourt, 2020.

Hallowell, Edward M. *Dare to Forgive: The Power of Letting Go and Moving On.* Simon & Schuster, 2004.

Chapter 6

Tutu, Desmond. *The Book of Forgiving: The Fourfold Path for Healing Ourselves and Our World.* Harper One, 2014.

https://www.britannica.com/topic/hindsight-bias

Chapter 7

Winch, Guy PhD. "5 Reasons Why Some People Will Never Say Sorry." *Psychology Today,* (29 May 2013). https://www.psychologytoday.com/us/blog/the-squeaky-wheel/201305/5-reasons-why-some-people-will-never-say-sorry

Coleman, Slash. "10 Ways to Apologize Appropriately." *Psychology Today,* (13 October 2013). https://www.psychologytoday.com/us/blog/bohemian-love-diaries/201310/10-ways-apologize-appropriately.

Chapter 8

Beiler, Anne. *Twist of Fath: The Story of Anne Beiler, Founder of Aunties Anne's Pretzels.* Thomas Nelson, 2010.

McMillian, J.M (2005). *How He Loves* (Performed by David Crowder Band).

Hedin, Eric R. PhD. *Canceled Science: What Some Atheists Don't Want You to See.* Discovery Institute Press, 2021.

Cola, J, Hayes, C, Lewis, H (1985) *Power of Love (Performed by Huey Lewis and the News).*

Chapter 9

The Gallup Organization. Washington, D.C.: Gallup Organization, 1999. https://news.gallup.com/poll/3874/nation-observes-national-day-prayer-pray-daily

Lambert NM, Fincham FD, Stillman TF, Graham SM, Beach SR. Motivating change in relationships: Can prayer increase forgiveness? Psychol Sci. 2010 Jan;21(1):126-32. doi: 10.1177/0956797609355634. Epub 2009 Dec 11. PMID: 20424033.

REFERENCES

Chapter 10

Kazdin, Alan E. *Encyclopedia of Psychology*. American Psychological Association, 2000.

Spielberger C.D., Krasner S.S., Solomon E.P. (1988) The Experience, Expression, and Control of Anger. In: Janisse M.P. (eds) Individual Differences, Stress, and Health Psychology.

Hanh, Thich Nhat. *Anger: Wisdom for Cooling the Flames*. Riverhead Books, 2002.

Contributions to Psychology and Medicine. Springer, New York, NY. https://doi.org/10.1007/978-1-4612-3824-9_5

Chapter 11

Hallman, Tom, Jr. "A Teacher, a Student and a 39-year-long Lesson in Forgiveness." The Oregonian: Oregon Live (22 April 2012). https://www.oregonlive.com/living/2012/04/a_teacher_a_student_and_a_39-y.html

Pink, Daniel. *The Power of Regret: How Looking Backward Moves Us Forward*. Riverhead Books, 2022.

Lerner, Harriet. Ph.D. *Why Won't You Apologize?: Healing Big Betrayals and Everyday Hurts*. Gallery Books, 2017.

Scher, S. and Darley, J. "How Effective Are the Things People Say to Apologize? Effects of the Realization of the Apology

Speech Act," Journal of Psycholinguistic Research, Vol. 26, issue 1 (1997).

Chapman, Gary and Thomas, Jennifer. *The Five Languages of Apology: How to Experience Healing in All Your Relationships*. Northfield Publishing, 2006.

https://www.mindtools.com/pages/article/how-to-apologize.htm

Segal, Erich. *Love Story*. Harper & Row (USA), 1970.

Hiller, Arthur. *Love Story*. Paramount Pictures, 1970.

Bogdanovich, Peter. *What's Up, Doc?* Warner Bros. 1972.

Chapter 12

Stevenson, David W. *Country Wisdom: What the World Can Learn from the Wit and Wisdom of the West*. Stoecklein Publishing, 2005.

Scharping, Dylan. *Amish Grace*. Lifetime Movie Network, 2010.

Pope, Alexander. *An Essay on Criticism, Part II*. Palala Press, 2016 (originally published 1713).

Conclusion

Chernoff, Angel. "10 Things to Remember Before You Take Things Personally." https://www.marcandangel.com/2021/10/24/10-things-to-remember-before-you-take-things-personally/

Godbey, Kelly. "Creating Your Ideal Life." Ideal-LIVING Magazine, Vol. 24, No. 1 (Winter 2022).

ACKNOWLEDGMENTS

First, I must thank my wife, Kimberly, and my daughters, Kylie and Kristyn. God alone knows just how many times I have had to say to them or, to put it more accurately, should have said to them, "I'm sorry, please forgive me." They have stood by me through thick and thin, and words alone can't express my appreciation for their love and support. I am hopeful that the writing and publishing of this book, on a subject I needed to learn, delivers life-transforming power for my family. Kimberly, Kylie and Kristyn, your support and encouragement through this process has been uplifting and inspiring. As Michael J. Fox once said, "A family is not an important thing, it is everything."

Writing a book can be a lonely and daunting challenge, but it cannot be written alone. I was blessed to have a fantastic team to help me throughout this project:

- Ellaine Usury, my writing and book publication coach. Your support, encouragement and expert advice on writing and publishing kept me on track and helped me push through the many challenges faced by a first-time author.
- Sky Rodio Nutall, editor extraordinaire. Your feedback and technical editing skills proved instrumental in turning a rough draft into a real book, and your generous comments on my written words helped build my confidence to complete this project.
- Chip Van Pelt, my book cover designer and fellow rock and roller. You are truly a soulful rocker whose talent

at the microphone and designing never ceases to amaze. Thank you for putting the icing on this book with a top-notch cover design.

- Alejandro Martin, at Bloom Design Agency, thank you for formatting this book for me. I had no clue what I needed, but you walked me through the necessary steps and produced a world class formatting for the book.
- My Launch Team, you know who you are. Thank you from the bottom of my heart for stepping up and helping me launch this book. To be honest, writing the book was a lot easier than publishing it, but your commitment to stepping up to support the Launch means the world to me.

I could not have published this book without the special assistance of my daughter, Kristyn Schott, who not only helped with editing but also helped me recruit a launch team and taught me how to use social media get the word out. Please check out her book, *More than Conquerors*, an exceptional devotional for women of all ages who struggle with any kind of eating disorder.

I am especially grateful for the many people who contributed in some manner to my decision to write this book, including Pastors John Stickl and Jason Hillier of Valley Creek Church. Your passionate preaching stirred the waters of creativity, and parts of this book exist only because of your Jesus-focused, Spirit-filled, Life-giving words echoing in my soul as I sat down to write.

Thank you to Pastor Jeff Warren at Park Cities Baptist Church. Your sermon on forgiveness sparked ideas that made their way into this book

ACKNOWLEDGMENTS

To my friend, Derek Weinbrenner, who never failed to ask, "How's the book coming?" Thank you for holding me accountable. You never ceased reminding me to fulfill this call.

Clayton Furry and David Whiting, I am indebted to both of you for your honesty, transparency, and support during our weekly Circle meetings. Thank you both for being there.

Others who have earned my gratitude include Pam Fenn, whose random distribution of a bible verse card led to a not so random decision to start writing, and Tiffany Ashley, who randomly shared a quote on forgiveness (unaware that I was even writing this book). One thing I have learned is that there is no such thing as randomness when it comes to answering the call of our Creator.

Last but not least, I am grateful for a loving and forgiving God, who modeled the very essence of forgiveness through the life, death, and resurrection of His Son and our Savior, Jesus Christ. The life-transforming spirt of forgiveness is available to each of us only because You have forgiven us and are calling us to forgive others. May we all heed Your call.

CAN YOU HELP?

Thank you for reading my book!

I really appreciate all of your feedback, and I love hearing what you have to say.

I need your input to make the next version of this book and my future books better.

Please leave me an honest review on Amazon letting me know what you thought of the book.

Thanks so much!

Steve

stevemschott@gmail.com

Made in the USA
Middletown, DE
25 October 2022